AF487954

HONEST

A MEMOIR OF
WHAT I BUILT, WHAT I LOST,
AND WHO I BECAME

MYESHA CHANEY

Published by Second & Sixth Media, Irvine, California

ISBN: 979-8-9948113-7-5 (hardcover)
ISBN: 979-8-9948113-2-0 (eBook)
ISBN: 979-8-9948113-6-8 (paperback)

First Edition

For my children,
who watched me rebuild
brick by brick.

You are my anchor.
I love you.

And for every woman
who chose herself
before she knew
if she would be understood.

AUTHOR'S NOTE

This book was not written to persuade, instruct, or explain. It was written to tell the truth.

What you will find here is not a linear story of loss and recovery, but a lived experience of becoming. Some moments are quiet. Others disruptive. All of them mattered.

I offer this story as it is, without apology or performance, in the hope that it meets you where you are. Take what resonates. Leave the rest.

CONTENTS

PROLOGUE

I had finally gotten to sleep in. It was 11:31 on a Saturday morning, and I had just started preparing a late breakfast when I received a text message.

It was from him. He wrote that he would be sharing a very long, carefully crafted statement about our divorce, which he included. For eighteen years, we had publicly held ourselves up as an example of what a healthy, successful Christian marriage looked like. To many people, our marriage had become a public symbol of stability, faith, and success. Our partnership represented true love, hope, stability, and faith in God. What would it mean now?

He followed his nearly three-page statement by inviting me to church for prayer the next morning. I stood there in my kitchen, eggs cold on the counter, and something in me went still. *This is really happening.*

What I did not say yet, what I could not afford to say, was the truer sentence rising underneath it: *This is over.*

Tears suddenly filled my eyes as the truth pierced through the numbness I had been living in. Our marriage was really ending, and this was the moment I had dreaded for months. It was time for the church to find out.

I stared at his message, unable to fully absorb what I read. I kept asking myself the same questions over and over. *How is this happening now? How could this be my life? How did we get here after so much time, energy, and prayer?*

My thoughts were interrupted by a sudden flood of calls and text messages:

"I am so sorry."

"I am here for you."

"Are you ok?"

I was confused at first; I had no idea what people were talking about. Then came the next wave of messages, the public announcement, the church email.

I froze. His statement, the one I had received an hour earlier, had already been posted on all his social media pages. It had been posted on the church's social media pages. It had been emailed to the entire congregation.

Everyone now knew the truth of my broken marriage. Everything I had fought to protect and present as whole had been exposed. The image of perfection I had worked so hard to cultivate throughout my entire life collapsed in an instant. The illusion was gone.

The more my iPhone chimed, the more real the moment became. I felt my heart pounding through my chest. I felt the blood drain from my face. The shame came first, then the humiliation, then the heartbreak that took my breath. I unraveled.

My legs gave out beneath me, and I hit the floor on my knees. A sound came out of me that I did not recognize. It was raw and primal, a cry pulled from a place beyond language. I screamed from the center of my pain, from the center of all the things I had buried, from the center of the life that was ending.

My kids came running. They found me there on the floor, shaking and crying in a way I had never done in front of them. They touched my shoulders and asked, "Mom, what's wrong?"

But I could not speak. The words would not come. When I finally managed to, the only thing I could say was, "It's all over social media."

My children were witnessing the end of my marriage and the end of my silence. What they saw that day would shape how they understood truth, safety, and courage long after the details faded.

It was a death. A spiritual one. It was the death of the woman I had been trained to be, of the life I had performed, of the illusion I had protected. My worst fear had unfolded in real time, in front of my children, in front of my community, and in front of the world. That was the price of a life built on silence.

I had been hiding my lived experience of my marriage for nearly two decades. I was hiding parts of myself, my hurt, my desires, and the woman I was meant to be. I had lived inside a story that demanded my silence and rewarded my sacrifice.

And now everything was out.

I could not undo it. It was too late to cover it. I could no longer pretend; the truth was no longer something I carried privately. It was exposed and it was loud.

The shame felt unbearable. I wanted to disappear. I searched for a way to escape the humiliation, the overwhelming grief, and the questions that flooded me. I wanted to erase this moment. I wondered how could I erase myself from this situation completely.

Maybe the only way out was not to feel any of it at all.

But I knew the truth. The only way out was through, and the only way through was to feel. It was time to feel everything I had avoided and even numbed. I needed to feel the weight of my own story—while the world watched.

I lay on that kitchen floor, broken open, and understood something I had never allowed myself to say out loud. I had been dying in that marriage long before it ended. The collapse was not the destruction of my life. It was the exposure of a truth I had been carrying almost imperceptibly for years.

I eventually stood up, but I moved as if my body had aged decades in minutes. I walked through the house, noticing everything with a new kind of clarity. The sunlight on the walls. The quiet in the rooms.

The way the air felt different now that I was no longer pretending.

Every piece of furniture looked familiar, yet nothing felt the same. The house had become a museum of the life I used to live. That life was built on endurance and established on presentation. Its foundation rested on me holding everything together by myself.

I paused in front of the hallway mirror. I saw my reflection, but she was not the woman I had been that morning. Something had fallen from her. The mask. The role. The weight of pretending. Her face looked devastated yet honest. There was pain in her eyes, but also clarity. She looked human for the first time in a long time.

I touched the mirror and whispered something to myself that I did not expect: "You are still here."

I said it again. Then, "You are still here. Your worst fear has come upon you, and you didn't die."

I did not know what the next day would bring. I had never considered how to rebuild a life that had come apart so publicly. What would it look like to face the community, the church, the expectations that had shaped my identity for so long?

But I was alive. Something had ended—and something had begun. It wasn't simply a new chapter, a new role or a new image to perform.

It was a return.

A reckoning.

A slow, painful rebirth.

I walked back to the window and watched the sky settle into the evening. The world outside moved on as if nothing had happened. Cars drove by. A neighbor watered his plants. A child rode a bike down the street. Life continued without acknowledging my loss.

Yet in that ordinary stillness, I felt something sacred. I felt the faintest spark of myself returning, like embers under ash. Quiet, but alive.

My old life died on that kitchen floor. The woman I had pretended to be died with it, and the woman I was becoming stood trembling in the quiet, facing a truth she could finally feel. The world might have learned about my divorce in a matter of seconds, but the truth of my life would take time to tell.

This is the beginning of that truth.

SURVIVAL AND FORMATION

THE LIFE I WAS TRAINED TO LIVE

Being the pastor's wife at a local church is an unusual role: after getting married and showing up on Sunday, there is no rite of passage. No orientation. No moment where someone explains what is expected of you or how to survive what you are stepping into. In the early years of my marriage, I was learning how to survive a role I had not yet learned to question.

One day I was living my life, and the next I was assigned a title and ushered into a world with strict rules I was never given. There was no manual, no rulebook, yet everyone else in the community seemed to know the unspoken expectations of their new "First Lady." These are never stated, only enforced. When you are a pastor's wife, you learn you have crossed a line when you fail to perform. A smirk, a look, a conversation overheard—that is how the feedback comes.

Before everything unraveled, before the quiet betrayals stacked up in my body, there was beauty. Real beauty. Being married and a new pastor's wife was stressful, but it felt golden, God-touched, and full. A life I loved and a life that loved me back; or at least, I believed it did. Before I tell the truth about what broke, I need to honor what was breathtaking.

My husband and I felt like best friends. For much of our relationship we worked as a seamless duo, a true partnership. I would sing, and then he would speak. The rhythm worked. People responded to us. Together we shared countless meaningful moments. We traveled the world side by side: the south of France, Bora Bora, Prague. Every summer brought new places, new food, new memories. Each year for our wedding anniversary,

I planned a trip just for us. We climbed the ladder of influence together, rising steadily into a life that felt expansive and affirmed. It felt good to be known in our community, and it was fulfilling to be respected.

It was a meaningful season of service. I was able to use my gifts fully, and I did that work alongside my spouse. We were young, African-American, and honored to have work that was genuinely positive. I believed we had real chemistry; we talked, we connected, we worked well together, and we invested deeply in our public relationship and shared persona. We had nearly two decades of good decisions. I never read or heard anything negative about us, and protecting that reputation felt non-negotiable. I was a full participant in the shared fantasy.

Fundraisers. Esteemed events. Red carpets. Press junkets. Travel. The experience of a lifetime—I felt privileged, lucky, blessed to live that life and to have a partner in it. We raised our children together. We started businesses together. We made money together. Our worlds were completely intertwined. We counseled other couples; we walked with people through pain. We stood in hospital rooms with families as they said good-bye to their loved ones, where I used my background as a registered nurse to help people understand what was happening when words failed them.

It was a privilege to choose each other, day after day. We were a power couple; many of our highest accomplishments were tethered to one another. Buying the new church venue was one of the greatest feelings of my life: raising the capital, closing the deal, remodeling it, seeing it featured in the press. We gave away millions of dollars through city partnerships. Our relationship represented legacy, roots, continuity—and then starring on a national reality television series together became its own affirmation.

I was *enough*. I had made it. My marriage confirmed that I was wanted, that I had worth, that I belonged. I was a part of more than just a church or a ministry; this was my calling, my chance for leadership. It gave me my voice. In this playground season of my life, I learned how to speak publicly, how to run a successful multimillion-dollar business, and how to move power, influence, and resources. All of this represented leaving the poverty I grew up in and building a life with security, purpose, and meaning. I had a beautiful new family, a home in a nice area, and a Mercedes in the driveway.

But I was only twenty-one when we married, and I had three children soon after. My children learned this life before they had language for it. They watched me carry joy and exhaustion in the same breath and absorbed the lesson that love meant showing up no matter the cost.

What I could not see then was that this life required a version of me who never rested, never needed, and never asked to be held. Maintaining it meant managing my tone, my emotions, my needs, my desires. Being useful instead of being known. I was loved for what I carried, not for who I was.

It did not feel like sacrifice at the time. I experienced it as devotion. I believed this was what it meant to be faithful, to be chosen, and to be worthy of everything I had been given. Only later did I understand that what I was living was not unique to me. It was a role with expectations larger than any one woman could hold.

From one congregation to the next, one thing is clear: the role of pastor's wife suffocates the woman living inside it. She is celebrated, admired, respected, and placed on a pedestal because of who she is married to. In the same breath she may be treated as less than human, tolerated, misused, gossiped about, and discarded. Whatever the pastor's wife experiences is highly dependent upon the tone of her husband, the main character in the entire religious movie.

Long gone were the stained-glass windows of the church I'd grown to know. By the time our ministry was well-established, church had shifted into a production-heavy experience with call sheets, timers, stage cues, and lighting design. There was security, reserved parking, and a carefully curated perception of the congregation's beloved leaders. Sunday after Sunday of standing backstage, mic'd up, getting last-minute beats from the stage manager before going out to minister to the people. My role as pastor's wife became a glamorous assignment heightened by the presence of my rock-star husband, though this is not reflective of ministry everywhere.

In the Black church, however, the role of a pastor's wife often leaves little room for personhood. You become an idea, a symbol, a soft landing place for the congregation's needs, fears, and projections. By the time I stepped fully into the role of First Lady, I had been trained to carry weight without ceremony, to protect the image, to make myself smaller so the life around me could appear larger. In this life, people look at you and see whatever they need: Strength. Grace. Perfection. Silence, when your truth is inconvenient. Your humanity becomes a luxury you are not allowed to afford. You swallow your own pain so the church can feast on your smile. You show up to serve while quietly tending to the hurts no one ever acknowledges.

There is an invisible hierarchy that governs you. Older women feel entitled to comment on your clothes. Younger women watch to see if you are worthy of admiration. Men treat you with reverence until they decide you should be quiet. Somehow, you are expected to carry all of it with unwavering grace. The Black church loves its First Ladies, but it can also consume them. It wants the glow without ever wondering what it costs to shine.

Before I could name it, something in me began to split into pieces. I learned to live in layers long before I understood the cost: my inner life, where I could be honest with myself; then the world I constructed, where I performed for love and approval; and then there was the messy, unscripted world I lived in every day. I became a master juggler of identities, both real and perceived.

When I went to church, I tried to let people see me as I truly was, but it was not safe. I was a figure to be admired, praised, and judged. Even though people were mostly kind, service and caretaking were their universal love language, and because I aimed to please, I gave these without limit. Sunday mornings were full throttle: I woke early, got myself and my children ready, and ensured every detail of the service was planned and executed. Leading worship meant early sound checks, but singing was the only place I felt fully seen. Between services I checked on volunteers, staff, children's ministry, parking, and logistics. I prepared my heart to worship again while managing everything else, and it was not even lunchtime. Afterward, I changed hats again: executive pastor, problem solver, the one responsible when things went wrong. Ensuring perfection became my protection.

Over time, what the church asked of me was nothing new. It simply gave a name and a platform to patterns I learned long before I wore a title. It formalized what occurred inside my marriage.

Even in motherhood, I carried more than was humanly possible. When teachers gently raised concerns about my young son, I felt the weight settle deeper into my body: ADHD. Anxiety. Words that explained his experience but did not lessen the daily labor. Homework stretched for hours while I learned how to manage meltdowns quietly, how to advocate without drawing attention. I carried it all mostly alone. I did not tell people for years. It wasn't something I was ashamed of, but the image we were protecting could not afford disruption. Silence felt safer than exposure.

On school days I managed everything: breakfasts, backpacks, appointments, schedules. I smiled, I performed, and when the day ended, I sat with my son and carried the invisible labor of his world without complaint. My love was proven through endurance, my worth through over-exceeding capacity.

Many of us are trained this way. We learn to take on more than is ours, believing the weight will eventually turn into security or affection. Endurance becomes identity, and identity begins to cost us.

Slowly, almost imperceptibly, the life I built became my prison. I believed that if I was chosen by my husband, I must be worthy. If I was needed by the congregation, I must be loved. If I could carry it all, I would eventually be held.

But what I experienced as power began to close in on me. The same calling that lifted me would one day consume me. Everything that later suffocated me was at first everything I ever wanted. I loved that life. I loved him. I loved what we represented. I loved the dream.

Losing it all—that was a form of death. It was not just a failed marriage. It was a fallen kingdom.

EVERYTHING I LEARNED ABOUT LOVE WAS SURVIVAL

The lie I lived by did not begin in my marriage or in the church. It began much earlier, in the house where I first learned what love required of me.

My dad was in and out of jail during my early childhood, and later I came to understand that he struggled with addiction that led to long absences from home. My mother raised me and my siblings as a single mother. She was patient, quiet, and a bit reserved. She spent time with her children and her family often, my grandmother and aunts. I enjoyed growing up around my extended family.

Mom did her best to take care of us. She made sure we were covered and protected. We lived in Section 8 housing, had food stamps, and received a supplemental welfare check. We had a house with three bedrooms and one bath. I thought it was a nice place to live; I didn't think anything negative about how I grew up during those years. We always had what we needed on a practical level. What we didn't always have was emotional consistency. This absence would quietly shape how I came to understand love.

While there wasn't an overwhelming struggle apparent, as a child, I knew there was more for me, and I was determined to get it. I was fiercely independent and craved space to roam and discover. Mom allowed me to go explore the city as early as twelve, make new friends, and have more responsibility. I would get on the city bus and go to the mall. With only five bucks to my name, I'd get Taco Bell, candy, and have bus fair to get back home. I demanded to change my name in the first grade after realizing it was not spelled phonetically correct. It was originally spelled Myishia, and I thought Myesha was easier to pronounce. After I made my case, Mom took me to change my name at the Social Security office.

My dad came home when I was in the fifth grade and stayed home for good. He would come home from work around 3:30 p.m. Some days there would be a banging on the front door. "Open this door," he'd shout. My heart would race. Even though I knew it could happen each day, I never knew when. I would hear his car approaching our street and anticipate needs. Was the kitchen cleaned? Check. Was my homework done? Check. Were his clothes laid out? Check. Like a tiny drill sergeant, I would go over anything I could think of that would trigger the old guy and remove it. On other days, I would have the door open. He would walk up the first long step to our house and be upset that I was in the house without the door locked. I couldn't win.

Somewhere in these formative years, I began to believe the idea that for me to be loved, I needed to do everything right. I followed the rules, overachieved, and caused very little stress to my parents. I was dutiful. Hard working. Polite. I was outgoing and smart. I loved getting straight As on my report card. I was also a performer at heart. My dad would often ask me to come sing for him and his buddies while they drank beers and smoked cigarettes. I couldn't wait until the next house party so I could show off a new song, my report card, or whatever else I was working on. I needed the affirmation, and I learned early how to get it. Whatever was needed, I had to provide. I needed to be the one. Some of this was my natural wiring. I believed that there was a strong connection between service and performance and me being accepted.

On the surface, I was just fine. Cooperative, easy to get along with and non-confrontational. On the inside, I took many steps back and withdrew emotionally into the abyss of my soul. It was not safe for me to relax. Dad was unpredictable. I never knew which person I would experience when he got home. He could be angry and physically intimidating, or he could be charismatic, generous, and exciting. I learned what it meant to live in dichotomy. I became hypervigilant. I studied my environment, scanned for threats, and adjusted my personality accordingly. If Dad was in a bad mood, I would be playful. I would cheer him up. If he was stressed, I would be good. I'd go the extra mile in cleaning, doing chores, or singing him a song. Whatever I had to do to ensure a peaceful home, I did it. This practice kept me safe, and it taught me how to hide way too young. Self-parenting learned too early often hardens into self-erasure later.

I lived in the paradox of thinking I need to do everything right to be loved and terribly afraid of getting in trouble or being punished. I didn't understand what whole, healthy love was. I knew my dad was there physically, but I couldn't always access him emotionally without the presence of fear or anger. I knew I was cared for and loved on some level, I just didn't have real proof or evidence of what that meant. There was only the emotional signature of absence *within* presence left on my soul. Love was there, but safety was conditional.

Growing up this way trained me in patterns I would carry forward. In my marriage, whenever I tried to share what I felt or needed, it turned into a critical discussion. It never felt like a conversation or a moment of curiosity, but an analysis. My words were examined, corrected, reframed. My tone was assessed. My timing questioned. My intent pulled apart until the original feeling was no longer recognizable. I learned quickly that speaking honestly required more energy than I had. It meant preparing myself for follow-up conversations, emotional fallout, long explanations, and eventual exhaustion. Silence was simpler. It cost much less. Over time, I stopped trying to be understood. I learned how to move around my husband the way I had learned to move around my father: Anticipating moods. Choosing timing carefully. Editing myself before I ever spoke. Saying things in ways that felt safer. Leaving other things unsaid entirely.

We called it friendship. And in many ways, it was. We talked often, we shared ideas, we laughed; we functioned well together. But it was one-sided. I knew his inner world intimately—his thoughts, his wounds, his struggles, but he rarely knew mine. Being known was not dangerous for him like it was dangerous for me. I learned early how to adjust myself, how to read a room, how to anticipate someone else's needs before they ever spoke a word. I knew how to perform safety, work for peace, and stay small so the storms around me remained manageable.

It's funny; I was married to a pastor, yet we rarely studied scripture together. We did not pray together in any consistent way. Early on it was decided that we would each have our own rhythms for how we studied, connected to God, and practiced our faith. At the time I told myself this was maturity, that faith was personal, that spiritual independence was healthy. Looking back, I knew something wasn't right about the spiritual temperature of our home. I couldn't admit that perhaps our entire life was built on a faulty religious foundation.

On Sundays I watched miracles unfold. People encountered God, and I did too. I stood in rooms where worship cracked people open, where prayers were answered, where lives shifted in real time. I believed in the power of God with my whole body. But at home, the character necessary to sustain that spiritual authority was absent. There was no shared altar. No shared submission. No shared humility. What was powerful in public did not translate into safety in private. That dissonance slowly eroded my understanding of God. I didn't lose faith, but I was living under a covering that did not feel like it had anything to do with faith. I was asked to trust a spiritual structure that did not hold me—to submit without being shepherded, and to honor what did not protect. Over time God began to feel distant in some ways because I no longer knew how to reconcile the husband I met in worship with what I endured at home.

Money was another place where responsibility fell on me and blame followed close behind. I grew up knowing what it felt like to have less, so safety, to me, meant planning, tracking, making sure nothing fell through the cracks. In our marriage I handled the finances while he rarely ever checked a bank account. He spent freely, on food, clothes, cars, trips, experiences. The card was swiped, life moved on, and every month, I sat alone at the table, figuring out how everything would be paid.

I was good at it; resourceful, strategic. I learned how to stretch, shift, cover, and absorb. But the problem was never the spending alone. It was that I carried the consequences in silence. When I could make it work,

I did, but when I couldn't, when the numbers no longer added up, I dreaded speaking.

Those conversations never went well. I would come forward with reality, and somehow I became the problem. How could I let it get this bad? Why didn't I say something sooner? I learned to live inside a double bind. If I solved it quietly, I stayed invisible, and if I named it, I was careless. He spoke often about the pressure he felt to provide, about the weight of leadership and responsibility, and yet there was no pause when it came to indulgence, no moment of restraint that said, *I need to protect my family.* I carried the math, the fear, and the risk, and then I carried the blame for it all.

As our life expanded and the pace of everything accelerated beyond what I could sustain, that same pattern returned in a way I could no longer minimize. Not long after our time on a reality show, a letter arrived in the mail that stopped me cold. It was from the IRS.

We were being audited for two years. I froze. Money had always lived close to fear for me, and I was the one who managed it all; I handled the taxes; I worked with the accountants. This would be mine and mine alone to solve.

For weeks my world narrowed to nothing but paper: receipts, buckets and binders, statements from years I could barely remember. Two of the busiest seasons of our lives—filled with travel, filming, ministry, and public responsibility—were suddenly reduced to documents that had to prove their innocence. I was exhausted before the meeting even happened. My hair was falling out, my skin was breaking down; I looked older than I was. My body knew what my mind was still trying to manage.

I showed up to the audit alone. It was me, the tax professional, and the auditor. We went line by line through my life. I answered questions, nodded, and tried to breathe steadily enough to stay present. At the end of the meeting a determination was made, and my husband and I were handed a six-figure tax bill.

I do not remember crying. I remember going quiet. The sensation of being cornered by responsibility I could not put down felt overwhelming. I had children, a church I was helping to run, a home, a ministry—a life that required me to keep moving no matter how afraid I was. And there was no one to tell: marriage and money were off-limits in every conversation.

I could not name how scared I was, so I learned to carry terror politely. That tax matter did not disappear overnight, but it was eventually resolved. What had once felt like a private catastrophe, something so large and shame-filled I could barely say it out loud, became one more thing I survived. We paid it. We handled it. And in time, what had terrified me most lost its power to define me. The fear was real, but it was not final.

It was still one of the lowest points of my life because it revealed I was doing the hardest things alone. It wasn't about me being strong; I did it because there was no one else to do them. That is not partnership, only survival. During this time something in me eroded. I realized I could no longer live inside a system where accountability flowed in only one direction. I wasn't asking for luxury, I was asking for integrity, though even that felt dangerous to name.

I would be lying if I said I had never sensed that something was wrong in my marriage. Deep inside, there had always been a quiet awareness that whispered, *This isn't right*. I ignored it because intuition without permission can feel irresponsible when you are young, hopeful, and trying to build something that resembles safety. As a child, I had never learned what real love meant; I grew up learning how to manage love instead, and I carried that through to my marriage. It happened early, in a season when feeling came before language. I was still learning how to override my body in the name of commitment. I didn't yet know how to name the discomfort or why my body registered danger before my mind could catch up. I only knew that something inside me began to contract quietly, long before I understood it as a warning.

But being known and being provided for are not the same thing.

Once I came across a set of flowers I loved. They were pale pink, soft, and intentional, exactly right for that season of my life. They were more expensive than most flowers, but they lasted a year. I imagined them in my home, seeing them every day, letting them quietly remind me that beauty could be chosen on purpose. I showed my husband. We talked about them, but I did not ask for them outright. I thought, *One day I will get those.*

When he surprised me with the flowers later, they were not pale pink. They were tan. Neutral, safe—and they cost twice as much.

I thanked him. I always did; gratitude came easily to me. But inside, something familiar settled into my chest. I had not been heard. I had been overridden.

That was the pattern. I received things I never asked for and then quietly figured out how to live with them, how to adjust, how to make sense of them. How to absorb the cost, financially and emotionally. From the outside, his actions looked like generosity, but from the inside, they felt like being edited out of my own life. That override became the emotional template of my marriage, teaching me how to disappear politely.

We planned a family trip to Hawaii. At the time I had two young children, and traveling felt overwhelming to me; I needed structure to feel safe, I needed help. He suggested that his mother come with us so she could assist with the children. I agreed. It made sense. And still, even before we boarded the plane, I felt crowded inside my own marriage in a way I could not explain.

The first night after we arrived, once the kids were settled and the room finally went quiet, he said he needed to go out and unwind. Drinking was not unusual for him; it had always been part of the landscape, but what followed that night was different. We argued over nothing of real importance. The conflict felt unnecessary, almost manufactured. I had learned by then that arguments were not something I could raise my voice in. They were something I had to minimize, something I needed to manage carefully so as not to escalate or provoke. I kept my tone steady, I chose my words with precision—and then he left.

I was alone in a hotel room I did not recognize, thousands of miles from home, with his mother and our children sleeping nearby. The walls felt unfamiliar. The air felt heavy.

I tried calling him. He did not answer. I called again. I was scared. I remember lying awake, staring at the ceiling, listening to the sound of breathing in the room and feeling the weight of responsibility settle onto my chest. I was holding everyone. The children, his mother—the whole night. He was gone.

That trip would become the moment my nervous system learned the rules of my marriage. I kept asking myself how a disagreement could end with disappearance, how conflict always seemed to resolve itself by leaving me alone to absorb the fallout, how easily my fear was dismissed by his absence.

When I woke up the next morning, he had returned. He was remorseful. He told me where he had gone, what he had done. He told me that he had been drunk, that he was not thinking. He told me he was sorry.

I listened. I nodded. I absorbed. And that was the first moment my body registered that something was wrong.

I recognized a familiar pattern of abandonment dressed up as normal conflict. In that moment, without being conscious of it, I learned something that would shape the next eighteen years of my life. His honesty would come to me privately, but silence would be my public responsibility.

After that night, I did not confront the fracture. I built over it.

I knew my role without it ever being spoken. I would contain the truth; I would make sense of it on my own. I would protect the story from becoming something other people could see. I would manage the damage quietly so life could continue without interruption. Leaving would have required naming a truth I was not yet willing to carry in the open. I did not leave, and I did not tell anyone. I folded the moment into myself and carried on.

This is how many of us survive what we don't yet have language for. We don't confront it; we store it. We believe that covering over the fracture will keep life moving forward. What we don't realize is that nothing we bury disappears. It simply relocates, settling quietly into the body, the heart, the soul, waiting to be felt again.

On the other hand, it's important to note my family never left me. They showed up in the ways they knew how: phone calls that stretched late into the night, drop-ins that grounded me, meals where I could sit quietly and not explain myself. They did not push. They trusted me to share what I could, when I could. They loved me steadily, without conditions. And still, I felt alone in ways I could not yet explain. I had not named what was happening as a *problem*. I was still inside it, functioning, and believing that endurance was faithfulness. My family were present, offering protection, but I did not yet know what I was carrying.

Before everything fell apart, I tried to give myself back emotionally to the marriage in the most honest way I knew how. This was before clarity, finding the language I have now, and understanding the cost of yielding without being met. I had begun doing deeper spiritual formation work, and something in me was waking up. I could see my patterns, and I started to understand how much of myself I had learned to suppress. I believed that if I came forward with humility and truth, we could begin again.

I wrote him letters. There was no accusation, ultimatum, or demand. I was careful, prayerful, measured. I chose my words the same way I always had: with reverence for God, for marriage, for the life we were building. I believed that sincerity would be enough, so in one letter, I wrote about my fear of standing on the edge of a season I did not yet understand. I told him I was afraid of disappointing him, afraid of losing what we had built, and afraid of asking for space to explore the parts of myself that were stirring back to life. At the same time, I told him I was willing to yield to what God was asking of me even if it cost me something I loved.

In another letter, I wrote about submission. About not being enough on my own, about trusting God to carry what I could not. I asked for help, for partnership, for people to be sent into our lives to support the vision we were holding together. I wrote about hope too, about wanting to enjoy each other as husband and wife, as parents, as friends, and about believing we could walk forward together in this season if we stayed open and honest.

Reading those words now, I am struck by how much I was offering and how little I was asking for in return. I was not praying for escape or for freedom. I was asking to belong.

But devotion without mutuality becomes self-erasure. I knew how to yield; I did not yet know how to be met.

Something in me began to thaw when I gave myself to deeper inner work, and for the first time, I could see myself even more clearly. The awareness was both liberating and painful. Needs surfaced that I had trained myself not to see, longings I had dismissed, desires I had learned to spiritualize away. I didn't yet know why I had ignored them for so long, but something had shifted. I had language now, tools for the work ahead, and I believed change was possible. Wherever I noticed myself shrinking, I began to stand up. Honestly.

One night, high above the city in a Japanese restaurant, I opened up to him deeply. I cried because I wanted to give my whole heart to my husband. Before, when I felt hurt, I had learned to retreat emotionally. This time was different. I wanted to rededicate myself, freely. I remember thinking, *This is it. This is where I can stay.*

For a moment, he met me there. He tried; it really felt sincere. But it did not last. Not long after one of the most hopeful seasons we had ever known, everything descended again. In the middle of that darkness, I asked a question I had been afraid to ask for years: "What do you love about me?"

He paused, then said, "I love how you love me."

I still do not know how to hold that answer. I do not know what he loved about my mind, my presence, my spirit, apart from what I provided. There was no evidence that the love he had for me did not also benefit him. I thought I was loved. I just could not find the proof.

My life was the most perfect external creation I could ever make. I made a promise when I met my husband that I would never mess our relationship up. I just knew I would do everything right and be the absolute perfect spouse because I thought I had won a prize. I believed that I was a part of a new world, a new family. I didn't realize I was trying to outrun an old wound, not fully step into love.

My husband held a senior leadership role in a prominent Black church in our city. The family he came from was deeply respected, long admired, and surrounded by a kind of reverence that felt inherited rather than earned. Every Sunday morning the family matriarch arrived impeccably dressed, carrying herself with quiet authority. It felt like a privilege to be welcomed into that world. They were widely admired, spoken of with warmth and esteem. Somewhere in my head and heart I had carried a story that I would be rescued from my life. I secretly wanted someone to come and sweep me off my feet, and with the arrival of my husband, my chance had finally come. I wanted out of the hood and far away from my old childhood identity. I wanted a life of abundance, safety, and security.

I entered that marriage carrying a lifelong hope that someone would save me. I was looking for a covering, a shelter, a place where I could finally exhale, and I believed that stepping into his world meant stepping into safety, that marrying into his legacy would rewrite my own. Somewhere deep inside, I thought proximity to his name, his church, and his family could heal the parts of me that had learned to live afraid.

I wanted belonging so desperately that I convinced myself I had found it. I told myself that if I stayed grateful and worked hard enough, if I kept the image pristine and the story intact, love would reveal itself fully one day. I confused access with acceptance and responsibility with intimacy. I mistook the weight of the role for the weight of being chosen. And yet, even in those early years, I felt the quiet whisper that something was off. I just buried it under worship lyrics, church programs, community work, and the applause of people who only knew the surface of who I was.

Holding on felt easier than grieving the life I thought I was being brought into. I poured myself into that life like it was a calling. I became the version of myself that the church needed, the city admired, and the cameras could capture. There was a thrill in it, a sense of purpose that wrapped itself around my wounds and made them feel holy. Every accomplishment felt like proof that I had made the right choice, that I belonged in this world I had adopted as my own.

My life was becoming larger, louder, more visible. Opportunities came. Platforms opened. Influence grew. The girl who once stood in Section 8 housing, looking for a way out, suddenly found herself right in the center of everything she thought meant she had finally arrived. It was that desire for more, that hunger to be seen and affirmed, that carried me straight into moments that felt like destiny, moments that convinced me I had stepped into the life I was meant to live.

What I mistook for destiny was familiarity dressed up as promise. And familiarity had always felt like home, even when it hurt.

THE COST OF BEING SEEN

There were seasons of my marriage that were genuinely good—moments of laughter, shared dreams, long conversations, satisfying intimacy, and the comfort that comes from building a life with someone you believe is committed to you. There were also seasons that devastated me in ways I felt more than I could explain. And then there was the long, quiet middle where most of life actually took place. That middle is where the real cost accumulated.

From the outside everything looked steady, productive, purposeful. We were building something meaningful. But inside the walls of our marriage, I was carrying weight that had no place to put down. I stayed composed while holding things that could not be resolved, repaired, or named publicly. Over time I became the place where every broken thing was brought, but nothing was healed.

My husband told me things the way other people confess to clergy: late nights, bad decisions, lines crossed and then dismissed as mistakes. He always told me. He said the Holy Spirit was grieved, so I never had to discover anything on my own. There were no secrets uncovered, no evidence stumbled upon, no public unraveling. And because he told me, I believed that made it intimacy. I believed honesty alone meant closeness, that being trusted with the truth was the same as being chosen—that the act of telling meant accountability had already occurred.

Confession without repair does not create closeness. It creates containment.

I absorbed what he could not hold. I regulated my voice, I quieted my questions, I took pain into my body and turned it into calm so life could continue uninterrupted. I learned how to translate discomfort into something that resembled peace. Nothing had been healed, but everything still had to function. I did not have to look for my disappointment; it found me.

I told myself this was partnership. It felt familiar, like a story I had watched play out before. Perhaps this was grace. I even told myself strong women do not flinch. The role trained me to measure my worth by my capacity to endure.

We were asked to lead a couples retreat once. These invitations were not unusual; on paper, we made sense together, though preparing for these events was often awkward. We approached meaning differently. My husband spoke with confidence, articulate and grounded in doctrine. I spoke from lived experience, from the interior places people rarely named out loud. He focused on how things should sound; I wanted them to feel human. We tried to find a rhythm that allowed both of us to be present, even when our instincts collided.

When it was my turn to speak, I shared something simple, something domestic, something true. I told the couples that in our bedroom, my side of the room was orderly: clothes folded, shoes put away, clear space. His side was not. Each day he removed his suit, his pressed clothes, his carefully chosen shoes, and left them where they fell. For years I had quietly picked everything up. I hung the clothes, cleared the space, and absorbed the responsibility without comment—until one day, I stopped. I decided that if he did not want to hang up his clothes, that was his choice, but it did not have to become my work. The bedroom now reflected that decision: my side remained calm and cared for while his side accumulated in piles.

I shared this as an example of how marriage does not require sameness to function, of how compromise can look like allowing difference without resentment. I thought it was a good illustration of how love does not require erasing yourself to maintain peace.

I spoke warmly. I spoke with care, without mocking him; it was never about criticizing him. I did not anticipate any sort of reaction.

Afterward, my husband was angry.

He told me I had embarrassed him, that I had disrespected him in front of his colleagues, that I had exposed something private that reflected poorly on him. And his reaction did not pass quickly. It followed us home, it resurfaced in arguments; it returned long after the moment itself had ended.

That single story became evidence, proof that my voice carried risk. It was never about clothes, or mess. It was about who controlled the narrative.

I began to second-guess myself. I didn't lack clarity, but I knew clarity carried consequence. I learned that I could speak only as long as what I said aligned with the version of me that protected his image. The acceptable range of expression sounded like nothing but admiration.

That lesson repeated itself in ordinary moments too. Once we were on vacation with friends, talking loosely about social media. Someone mentioned Twitter. My husband said he did not like it. I added that I did not enjoy it either, that it felt like a space built on constant debate and quick exchanges. "Twitter is for smart people," I said. What I meant was that it intimidated me, that it felt sharp and fast, like a room where everyone except me knew the language. I did not feel fluent there. This was not a judgment; it was a confession disguised as an opinion.

That comment followed me for years. I was told it was embarrassing, that it made it seem like I was saying he wasn't smart, and that it revealed something unkind or careless about me. The moment was replayed and reinterpreted. My intent was replaced with his negative rendition of what I had meant. I came to understand that even small expressions could become permanent evidence.

Certain versions of me were affirmed while others carried a cost. When I spoke in ways he enjoyed, approval followed, so over time, I learned to represent instead of reveal, to manage instead of author. What I could not name at the time was this: visibility alone is not power. I was present, admired, even celebrated, but I did not control the terms of my presence.

I could be seen as long as I stayed within a version of myself that served the system I was in. Visibility gave me access, but it did not give me autonomy.

✳✳✳

By the time the annual culture fest arrived, I had learned how to operate inside those limits. I knew how to show up composed, articulate, and radiant while privately carrying what had no room to exist. It had become easy to convert pain into performance and call it strength. When I stepped onto the red carpet, the applause no longer simply felt like affirmation—it felt like oxygen.

We had just been on a reality television series centered on pastors and their families—the first of its kind, and it gained attention quickly. That year the cast traveled south for a press run at an annual culture festival. The convention center was packed with people who loved their favorite television pastors. As we moved toward the stage, police escorts cleared space. People reached out, calling our names, asking for photos and autographs. We moved through private corridors. Car service waited outside. We had access to many exclusive parts of the fest. I wore a royal blue Ted Baker jumpsuit, and my hair fell down my back in long, dark waves. I had lost more than twenty pounds and felt at home in my body. It was bright and loud, and my system buzzed with adrenaline.

Someone asked how it felt to be there. I laughed and said, "It's surreal." But as I stood there, something in my body tightened. My throat burned. I suddenly became aware of how much effort it was taking me to remain composed. The visibility was intoxicating, but my body knew something my mind was still catching up to: access is not the same as safety.

What I did not say was the quieter truth forming underneath: *If this is the peak, what would it cost me to stay here?* In this moment I felt taller, less apologetic, and I knew that whatever had awakened in me would not survive being folded back into a version of myself that existed by permission.

More than fifty media outlets lined the red carpet. I began the interviews standing next to my husband; that was the expectation. Then a photographer asked to take photos of me alone.

I stepped forward.

I smiled.

I let myself enjoy it.

For a few hours, I was not anyone's wife. There was no role to play; I was not lost in responsibility. I was *myself*. In that light, something inside me stirred.

Even there, I could feel the limit. The attention was real, but the terms were always present, hovering just outside the frame. I could be seen only as long as I did not claim authorship over who I was becoming.

The culture fest clarified something I had been avoiding: I did not want visibility that required permission. I wanted a life I could stand inside without negotiating myself smaller.

I was seen everywhere, but I did not yet belong to myself.

WHEN LOVE LOOKED LIKE SALVATION

I was young, searching, and quietly convinced that love would fix what I did not yet know how to hold on my own. I wanted my happily ever after: the white picket fence, a little dog, two children, and a husband who would choose me fully and forever.

That longing had been forming since my preteen years. I did not desire a casual love; I wanted a love that would organize my life around it, a love that would give shape to my days and meaning to my effort. I imagined myself being chosen with certainty, no hesitation, and loved without having to convince, prove, or perform. I believed this kind of deep, true love as opposed to the kind of love I had growing up, would finally let me exhale.

Even while I focused on accomplishments—good grades, competition, and performance—between winning awards and a standing ovation for my rendition of Maya Angelou's "Still I Rise," my thirteen-year-old self would often wonder, *Who is going to love me?* No amount of achievement satisfied my desire to be accepted, understood, and wanted, but I kept right on building a life that worked on the outside while my longing for love grew louder underneath it.

I did not see my ambition and my longing as connected; I thought they were parallel tracks. One was about purpose, and the other was about love. I did not yet understand how easily achievement can become a substitute for intimacy or how quickly success can quiet questions it never actually answers. Through high school I stayed busy and successful, but I did not date much. I was careful and guarded. I wanted love, but I did not trust that it was safe to want it openly. I could be surrounded by people and still feel alone. I was growing in many areas of my life, but intimacy felt underdeveloped.

At eighteen I graduated high school full of hope. The world felt open as I applied to colleges. I drove myself every Sunday to the same church I had attended since childhood where I sang in the choir and joined the worship team. My faith felt alive, sincere, and central to who I was becoming., so not long after committing to the worship team, I prayed a simple prayer: *Please send me the person I am supposed to spend my life with. Amen.*

Two weeks later, I attended rehearsal and saw him standing there, sharing his vision. Beautiful, confident—and familiar. I remembered seeing him occasionally throughout my childhood. He lived in another city and had recently returned home from college to help with leadership at our church. He was four years older than me.

We began rehearsing together, singing on Sundays and spending time together with the rest of the worship team. One day the whole group planned a trip to the movies. I arrived on time, excited—but when I walked up to the theater, he was the only one there. Everyone else had cancelled.

It became our first date.

It felt magical. Effortless, like something clicking into place. Nothing was complicated; there was no ambiguity to navigate, no tension to hold. The simplicity itself felt like confirmation. Many years later, I would realize I mistook ease for alignment and clarity for compatibility, but what I hadn't discovered yet at the tender age of nineteen was that relief often feels like revelation when you have been aching to be chosen for a long time.

I did not fall in love with a man as much as I fell in love with the *sensation of being chosen.* All the years I had spent feeling unclaimed suddenly felt redeemed. I interpreted the timing as divine; it seemed as though God really had answered my prayer that quickly!

What I called love in this season was not intimacy. It was relief—the sudden peace after years of wanting. I no longer had to wonder if I would be chosen. But this was the absence of longing, not the presence of deep knowing. I mistook the peace of being chosen as safety—and safety for love. At the time, the distinction felt impossible to discern, but now I know it mattered.

I did not fall in love because I was deeply known. I fell in love because the wanting stopped. And if God had sent him, then staying must be faith. That was the logic I lived by. Relief can be mistaken for destiny when longing has gone unanswered for a long time. Rest alone can feel like safety when you have never been taught how to tell the difference between the two, and when romance looks like salvation, you do not question it.

You surrender to it.

THE WOMAN WHO HELD EVERYTHING

I often felt like Cinderella: not in the fairy-tale sense, but in the quiet economy of obligation that governed my life. To be fair, I had built this world myself, and for a long time, I did not resent the weight of it. I cooked, cleaned, managed the house, cared for the children largely on my own, navigated my child's early ADHD diagnosis, and spent hours helping one child with homework while learning the needs of another—all while caring for a baby.

I woke before the sun and prepared for the day. Dinner was planned before breakfast. I got the children to school then headed to work at the church. I liked being the first to arrive; I took pride in modeling what I expected from the staff. I worked all day, picked the kids up, then returned for rehearsal. I sang, ran meetings, solved problems, and held everything together as it arose.

By this point years of marriage, leadership, and responsibility had layered themselves onto my body and my identity: I was the one who showed up, the one who handled what needed to be done without complaint. I was proud of my strength, my reliability, and my ability to execute. Competence became my currency. It was how I received affirmation, how I felt loved. Being overlooked through all of this did not register as a loss; I called ignoring it maturity, putting up with it sacrifice. I told myself this was what strong women did.

Until I realized it wasn't. And once the thought crossed my mind that there might be another way to live, I could not unsee it.

There were two people living inside me: The woman on the inside whispered, *Myesha, somehow, some way, God will work this out.* The woman on the outside showed up, delivered, and kept everything running. She crossed every *t* and dotted every *i*. Over time that split exhausted me; I wanted the woman *inside* to be seen. She had thoughts and needs too. She wanted rest, and she wanted to enjoy life in ordinary ways—to sit still, to watch movies, to sleep in on a Saturday.

But my role was to hold everything together so everyone *else* could rest. That dynamic lived not only in big responsibilities but in the smallest rituals, the ones repeated so often they felt normal.

One example stands out in my mind: My husband always looked impeccable. Pressed shirts, carefully chosen shoes, nothing accidental—his appearance intentional and curated, like a Sunday morning message. I did my best to keep up, but with children that small, perfection was rarely an option. Sometimes I brushed my hair quickly and chose my outfits for comfort and speed. After all, we were getting out the door alive. Wasn't that what mattered?

But repeatedly, as I stood getting dressed, he would glance at me and say, "You're wearing that?"

It was not criticism—not directly. It was a question. But questions become instructions when they are asked often enough and never challenged.

I would pause. Look back at myself. Feel something shift in my body. More questions would follow: about the fit, about the color, about how it might look to others . . . and suddenly I was changing. I didn't want to, but wearing what I had on no longer felt easy.

What confused me was how often this choice felt like my idea. I would walk out the door believing I had chosen differently, unaware how much the choice had already been shaped by him. Over time I learned to pre-edit myself, everything from my clothes to my words to my presence.

I thought I was managing optics, but I was also quietly dismantling my self-trust. The small exhilarations I once had slowly disappeared: the joy of choosing something because it felt like *me* and the satisfaction of trusting my own judgment. I learned to confer, to check, to defer and once I understood what was expected of me, I moved in sync. I could anticipate his response before it was spoken; I could correct myself before the question was asked.

That rhythm felt like peace. I *finally* knew how to move in the world. But it was actually the gradual outsourcing of my authority.

An inner critic took up residence in my mind—one that sounded reasonable, protective. It resembled the voice of wisdom. But it did not originate with me. Adjusting myself to its demands felt safer than risking the tension of standing still, resisting it. Relational harmony was not something I could ask my spouse for; it was something I had to contort myself to preserve.

At the time I did not experience this as control; I told myself it was consideration, keeping the peace. Partnership. Strong women adapted; that was what love required.

What I could not see was how often I disappeared before I ever arrived. Most of us are not trying to abandon ourselves. We are trying to survive.

The moment I could no longer hold it came without ceremony. I remember standing over the sink, washing dishes, tears falling into the water. I did not want to do this anymore, but I felt like I had to. I thought, *What is all this preaching and teaching for? What was all this prayer and fasting for? Because this does not feel like the life Jesus promised.* Something about it all felt off. Unjust. I had become so good at making everything look easy that no one could see how lonely I was, and I did not know how to ask for help.

I told myself this was the cost of being strong, but I had built a life that *looked* right only to realize it did not *feel* right. Everything I loved had been built on me disappearing, and healing would require questioning everything I had created.

In this moment, bent over the sink, I was not chasing some grand vision. I was looking for evidence that peace was real, that it existed beyond sermons and scriptures. Something inside me kept insisting that I was worthy of more.

For thirteen years I had chosen not to speak to anyone about my marriage. No mentors, no elders, no friends, no family. I carried everything alone and called it faith. I believed sacrifice was holy even when it was costing me my life. This was not cruelty; it was conditioning that worked too well. What was holding everything in place was not love. It was a contract I had never consciously signed. I had learned to survive by being indispensable, to stay chosen by staying useful, to keep peace by shrinking my own needs. Faith had fused with performance, and marriage became the structure where that belief could live unchecked.

I had not questioned it because it had worked—up until now. This system had produced stability, admiration, and purpose. But beneath the order I maintained so well, something essential was being withheld. The effort it took to keep this life intact was no longer undetectable to my body, and the cost of remaining in my marriage as it was had begun to outweigh the fear of what might happen if I left.

PROXIMITY

I did not go looking for another way of knowing. I had already been taught how truth was meant to show up: it came sanctioned by scripture, confirmed by authority, and tested by discipline. It required obedience, endurance, and suffering that could be measured and named as growth.

But something in me had begun to recognize a different kind of knowing. One that did not ask permission, one that did not wait until I was ready. It arrived fully formed and refused to leave once it had been felt. I recognized it in my body before I could situate it inside belief or explanation, and whatever was waking up inside me could not be contained within the life I was still living.

Around that same time, my husband and I arrived at an office for a tour. It was remodeled, clean, and professional: gray walls with a pop of blue throughout. It leaned more masculine than my taste, but it was well done, intentional, and polished. We were deep in renovations on the building we had purchased—navigating plans, builders, and decisions larger than anything I had ever managed before—and we needed a temporary office for our staff while construction was underway. Everything in my life at this time revolved around logistics, responsibility, and forward motion.

The woman who greeted us carried herself with ease. She was confident and grounded as she introduced herself and her husband, who was polite and well spoken, quieter than she was. They walked us through the space and explained the build-out: they had recently purchased an office nearby and were looking to sublet this one. We toured both options and soon realized one might be too large for our team and the other too small.

But while it was not perfect for the church office staff, the smaller office was perfect for me. We needed to figure out how we could make it work.

We sat down to talk. The woman smiled and said, "Y'all Black. We Black. What's up?" I relaxed immediately. This was the first time I had ever toured an office space like this, but we talked easily. They asked about our work, our goals, our story. I shared about my first project, *Hiding Behind the Lipstick*, how it began as a book and grew into a women's gathering that explored the ways we perform strength and composure while quietly carrying what we have not yet named. She loved what I was doing, and I loved creating spaces where women felt seen. But somewhere in that conversation, something else surfaced.

I rarely moved through the world as a singular person. Everything required coordination, agreement, and consideration. I felt a longing rise in me, not for the office itself, but for what it represented: a place that could hold my work and my becoming without negotiation.

It startled me how close that possibility felt.

I could imagine my desk there, my calendar on the wall, my chair. My rhythm. A door I could open and close without explanation. The smallest version of autonomy. The smallest version of *mine*.

I noticed how easily my body responded to the idea of returning to a place that did not already know me, a place where my presence did not arrive with expectation. The thought of entering a room without having to represent anyone else felt radical.

I had not realized how rarely I moved through spaces that were not already assigned meaning before I arrived, rooms where my presence did not need to support a narrative, places that did not ask me to uphold continuity. The office did not promise freedom, but it hinted at something more essential: choice.

I had lived most of my life *adjacent* to my own decisions. Close enough to influence them, rarely the one fully claiming them. Authority existed around me; ownership of myself belonged to someone else. I understood responsibility but not authorship. I knew how to keep things running without ever placing myself at the center of them. Proximity was my role. I had learned to hover at the edge of what mattered. I could read a room before anyone spoke, I could intercept tension before it became visible, and I understood how to protect stability, how to prevent rupture. My value lived in anticipation and containment. I was indispensable in practice but invisible in authority.

It wasn't just emotional suppression; it was systems maintenance.

The system rewarded it. Things ran smoothly, people felt supported, and the structure stayed intact. But it came with a subtle cost. I was relegated to staying just outside the places where decisions were made.

We submitted the application for the office space and provided the financial documents. It was a strong offer, but the office never became ours. They ended up renting it to someone who could lease both spaces.

I was disappointed, but something had already shifted. I began to see how often I had lived *near* my own life without inhabiting it. How easily I recognized what I wanted—and how practiced I was at standing just outside of it.

Around that same season, the woman from the office reached out and asked me to lunch. Our conversations were unstructured and unhurried. We talked about leadership, work, marriage, stress, and the parts of ourselves that rarely made it into public conversation. She lived outside the pressures that shaped my daily life. She moved without rehearsing, without bracing. She did not offer answers, but she did offer contrast.

Being near her showed me how much effort I spent maintaining alignment to forces outside myself. She did not organize herself around preservation of the status quo; rather, she adjusted when she needed to and trusted that movement would not collapse everything behind her.

I did not want her life so much as I wanted to understand how she inhabited it. How did she stand inside her choices instead of circling them? How did she trust her own center enough to live out of it? Clarity, I began to understand, does not always arrive as instruction. Sometimes it arrives as proximity to people who have already crossed a line you are still afraid to identify.

I began to notice how many people structure their lives while staying at the edges of them. They pour themselves into work they believe in, support relationships they value, and nurture visions of a future they can almost see. They are present, committed, and responsible, yet something essential remains unclaimed: they participate without inhabiting. They maintain without authoring. Proximity can feel like participation, it can feel like progress, but it is not the same as inhabiting what belongs to you.

The office may not have belonged to me, but the life it represented did. I had not been kept from that room so much as I had learned how to stand near what was mine without stepping fully into it.

THIS WAS SUPPOSED TO BE THE GOOD PART

After the height of the reality show, I stepped into what felt like one of the most confronting seasons of my life. This increased level of visibility would eventually expose everything I had been holding together. Having cameras in my home filming my children and watching my life play out on national television forced me into a mirror I could not escape. No one did anything wrong; the cameras simply showed me what I had learned to hide, and I did not recognize the woman I saw then. Something in me felt heavy, tired, older than I really was. I was still young, but I carried myself like someone who had been holding the world on her back for decades. In the years immediately following our time on television, my life may have appeared fuller, brighter, and more expansive than it had ever been, but the foundation beneath my marriage quietly eroded.

I was in my early thirties: a time of renaissance in more ways than one. On the outside I looked like I was coming into myself, but on the inside, something quieter and far more destabilizing was beginning to stir. I started filming scenes alone, carrying my own weight, not needing anyone beside me to interpret what I should or should not be doing. A self I had kept muted for years was beginning to surface. I could feel it rising. Every time I stepped onto a stage to share the message of *Hiding Behind the Lipstick*, I felt the truth moving through me: I had built a ministry to help women come out of hiding while I was still hiding inside my *own* life. It was surprising, ironic, and all too real.

During the week I managed the children, the house, and everything required of me at church, and on the weekends, I boarded planes and stepped into an entirely different world. Before long I realized that freedom had conditions. I could be myself when I was somewhere else—on a stage, in a hotel, in rooms where no one expected me to disappear—but each return home required me to fold myself back into place.

The contrast became impossible to ignore.

For most of my marriage anything I wanted for myself had to be translated into something that served us both. If I grew, we grew; if I moved forward, he moved forward. My ideas were acceptable just as long as they were shared, if they could be framed as "we," not "me." I had learned this instinctively. If I did something interesting or creative on my own social media, I made sure there was something parallel happening on his. If attention came my way, I redirected it back to him. If momentum built around my voice, I slowed it down to make room for my husband. I told myself this was unity. But one evening, walking down the street after dinner, I said something small but honest. It did not feel dramatic to me; it felt clear.

"For this next chapter, I want to do something just for me."

I explained to my husband that I loved speaking, I loved traveling, and I loved helping people, so I wanted to focus more intentionally on building my own brand. I wanted space to create without having to translate every idea into our shared benefit or mutual alignment. I wanted freedom to explore something that felt fun and alive and mine. To be clear, I was not asking for separation, nor was I rejecting our life together. I was simply naming a desire for autonomy—something I was learning every grown person ought to have.

His reaction startled me. What I experienced as clarity, he received as conflict. What I experienced as growth was interpreted as selfishness. What I experienced as honest communication turned into hours of questioning about my motives, my character, my implied lack of consideration—doubts about my faithfulness.

The conversation did not end when the walk ended. It expanded, followed us home, resurfaced later. It lingered. And something devastating became clear to me: I was not struggling to speak. I was struggling to feel safe in speaking.

Wanting autonomy was not a neutral topic, it seemed. It landed with my husband as a rupture. My desire to focus on something that brought me joy, creativity, and expression was destabilizing to my spouse. I felt confused when I realized this, ashamed and guilty for wanting something that felt, to me, fundamentally human.

Just like that, the pieces stopped fitting.

A God who created desire did not align with a marriage where desire was suspect. Partnership did not align with a structure where authority was fixed solely in one party. I was a helpmate whose own needs were treated like liabilities. Where was the love in this? What was rising in me wasn't rebellion; it was honesty. I wanted to move toward what made me feel alive without asking permission for it.

But no matter how pure my intentions, the guilt followed me. I had learned that goodness meant alignment, and alignment meant shrinking. By then, silence was doing the work faith had once promised to do.

That was the night I understood this clearly. The cost was not abstract; it exacted a toll on a body, and that body was mine. I would have racing thoughts and palpitations. That realization didn't send me folding inward this time; it drove me forward, back out. I was already traveling, already speaking, already holding space for women who were naming the same ache I was just starting to acknowledge in myself, only now I could feel that contrast in my nervous system. What was breaking me privately was clarifying me publicly. When I spoke, I was no longer speaking from theory or intellectual preparation; I was speaking from a life that was actively splitting in two. I did not have to manufacture new material because the message lived inside of me.

Women who heard me wept. They told their stories, they held their pain up to me like something sacred, and I knew God was meeting us in those rooms. I knew the work was true. For the first time, people saw me and said they valued *me*. They wanted *me*. They supported the work I was doing, by myself.

That mattered more than I knew how to explain. That year breathed life back into me. It gave me permission to take up space. I hired a nanny to care for things at home during those weekends. It was the first time I had ever put something in place to support my own life so I could step fully into something I loved. It was a radical step—once I took it, I could not pretend I had not. It told me I mattered enough to tend to my own life with intention. I had written something honest, and it felt to me as though God himself had breathed on it, growing it into a movement. I was not producing sermons, but I was telling the truth, and people were responding to the truth.

I wanted to sharpen my professional skills; I needed something solid enough to hold what was emerging in me. I wanted language, structure, and grounding for what I was already living, not merely more credentials. But when I told my husband what I wanted to pursue, I felt a familiar dynamic activate inside of me. I explained my desires carefully, framing them in terms of how they served the larger picture. Eventually I was given space to move forward. Once I did, I committed fully. I applied for seminary and I was accepted. That fall I walked into a classroom as an adult student in my thirties unaware of how much would now begin to unravel. The first core class was spiritual formation, and the opening lecture ignited something within me. The language the professor used around guilt, shame, hiding, and transformation gave words to a life I had been navigating instinctively. It was the first time I realized that spiritual formation is not about becoming *better*, but about becoming *honest*—and once honesty has language, it can no longer be negotiated.

I had been guiding women out of their places of hiding without having the words for my own. What I had grasped only at an intellectual level before now began to unsettle me relationally. At the same time, I was still speaking almost every weekend. I would leave on Thursdays, return late Saturday night, show up at church on Sunday, and begin again. I felt alive on the road, free, unguarded, and fully myself, but each return home sharpened the contrast. The domestic life I had built felt more constrictive. The stories I'd told myself to survive had hardened into the walls of a cage, and the effort it took me to maintain the perfect image at home was becoming harder and harder to ignore.

How do I stay committed to a life that no longer has space for who I am becoming? Even asking myself the question felt dangerous. It was not that I was trying to change him; I was trying to understand myself. I wanted to live without pretending, and I wanted to be loved for who I was, not who I performed to be, but the image I had spent years protecting had become the thing entrapping me. I smiled through interviews even as I began to feel the cost of staying.

Sometimes clarity bypasses the mind altogether; it enters through the body. Your pulse slows, your jaw releases, or it clenches, and something in you goes quiet. You suddenly understand, without explanation. No argument can undo this knowing, no logic can soften it. The knowing stays.

One night, I was not arguing. I was being spoken to. His voice escalated quickly, sharp and rapid, spilling words that did not hesitate before hitting me.

I stayed still, gray and silent, waiting for the storm to pass. He cursed me out fully, without restraint. "Fucking bitch! Stupid hoe!" The words were violent. Deliberate. Thrown to wound.

I did not respond. I had learned that responding only fed it, so I absorbed it. I waited. But inside me, something else was happening.

I was ten years old again, standing in my childhood body. Hearing my father's voice. Remembering the way I learned early that love and cruelty could live in the same house.

My only solace in that moment was a sentence I repeated silently to myself, the same sentence I had used to survive as a child: *You do not talk to someone you love like that.* I said it over and over inside my chest. I said it to keep my center, to remind the little girl within me that what was happening was not normal, even if I had normalized it. That sentence was the only place I could stand without falling apart.

And then something else happened. My daughter crawled out from under the bed.

She stood in the doorway, eyes wide, body fixed in place, watching. Taking it in. *Learning*, like I had learned, without needing any words.

The weight of it all landing on her hit me differently. This kind of treatment from my husband wasn't new to me. I knew how to survive it. I knew how to contain it, minimize it, move past it. I had done that for years.

But my daughter had not.

In that moment I understood what I could no longer carry. Silence does not only protect—it teaches.

My husband stopped yelling and went to her. His voice softened. I stayed where I was, watching the shift happen in real time as he started to explain in an attempt to comfort her. He led her out of the room. I didn't follow them.

I stood there with the truth settling into my bones: *This is no longer contained inside me.* Whatever I tolerated was being witnessed. Whatever I endured was being learned. That night marked the end of my ability to tell myself this was only affecting me. I could survive many things, but I could not survive teaching my children that love sounded like rage and safety required enduring abuse.

✳✳✳

Life continued while I searched for somewhere to put what I could not say. In the later years of my marriage, I coped the only way I knew how: every night, almost without fail, I ran a hot bath, closed the door, and disappeared into bubbles and books. This became my sanctuary. If you came to my house at eight o'clock at night, you would find me submerged in warm watersoft music playing and a stack of books beside the tub, trying to remember myself. It was there in the quiet, in the water, in the exhaustion that I ordered a book that would change everything.

I had been scrolling Amazon, half-present, numb, when I saw it sitting at the top of the bestseller list—glowing like it had been waiting for me. *Untamed* by Glennon Doyle.

I clicked *Buy Now* without thinking twice. I did not know what it was about; I only knew I needed whatever truth lived inside it. From the moment I cracked it open, something in me responded like it had been starving for years. I devoured that book, inhaled it, finishing it so quickly that I knew I would have to go back and read it again because my soul had swallowed the words faster than my mind could keep up.

I was fascinated by people like the author who were once deeply rooted in the church and then somehow found a way out. They didn't stop believing in God anymore, but something in their life shifted so drastically that the old container could no longer hold the truth of who they had become. Whenever I found a story like that, I paid attention. It felt like gathering evidence to witness people survive the kind of unraveling I feared was coming for me.

Glennon's story was riveting. She had been a Christian writer, married with children, before her entire life cracked open: she divorced her husband, fell in love with a woman, and rebuilt her life from the inside out. Reading her words was like being handed a map to a world I didn't know I was allowed to imagine. I was so lit up by the book that I told my husband about it—"This book is amazing!"—because it gave me the courage to accept a truth out loud.

But when I told him what the book explored, he told me it was *demonic*. That word landed in the room and did not move. He was concerned Glennon challenged values we both held at the time, and he didn't understand why her story mattered to me. I couldn't explain it then, but the truth is that *Untamed* wasn't telling me to burn down my life; it was telling me that if something must burn to save your soul, then the fire is holy. Glennon wasn't glorifying destruction, she was illuminating what happens inside a woman when she stops abandoning herself to keep the peace. Her words awoke something in me, something so small and tender I almost missed it. A whisper, a spark, a tiny flame of possibility . . . but I wasn't ready to go. I wasn't ready to name the cost of staying.

Yet reading this book had given me the words for questions I had been carrying quietly for years. I was still not ready to admit out loud that part of me wondered if staying meant the slow death of who I actually was, and Glennon's story gave me something I had never held before: permission. Permission to question, permission to imagine, permission to listen to my soul—permission to consider a life that did not cost me my own self.

I did not take that permission as a signal to leave, but as an invitation to try again differently. For a year and a half my only question for my husband was, "How can I be me and you be you and us still be together?" I wanted so desperately to find another way—a softer way, a way that didn't require burning anything down. I wasn't looking for a divorce. I didn't think I needed to escape, but I was trying to make the impossible possible.

All the same, that night as I submerged myself in warm water, the book resting against my chest, something settled inside of me: if the choice ever came down to abandoning myself or abandoning the life I had built, I was allowed to choose me.

I wouldn't act on that truth yet. But once it had arrived, it would rearrange everything it touched.

FRACTURE

THE DAY I STOPPED HOLDING IT TOGETHER

We were just finishing the building project that took nearly everything out of me. We were financing, building, and maintaining multiple realities at once, none of which could afford to fail. At the same time I had just completed two master's degrees in three years and had three school-aged children at home. On paper my life looked unstoppable, but in my body, I was past my limit.

Then the Covid-19 pandemic started, with the grand opening of the new church building scheduled for Easter. I had worked so hard to get the project completed, and now everything stopped. However, once the sheer panic subsided, I was secretly happy: I didn't have to perform the way I used to. *Yet while everyone rested, I continued working.* I had to keep everything afloat and move all our offerings into the digital space.

A few weeks after Mother's Day, my dad started bumping into walls when he walked. It wasn't dramatic at first—not the kind of thing you'd immediately recognize as an emergency, but something in the way his body shifted told the truth before anyone could name it. His left leg dragged just slightly, and his left arm hung a little heavier. When he tried to speak, the words caught in his mouth as though they were suddenly too big to fit through. One day my mom called me as she watched him try again to force a sentence out. When I heard the strange slur in his voice, I felt my stomach drop through the floor. My mom tried to act calm, but I could hear the panic in the way she called his name, the way she hovered near him like she was ready to catch him if he fell. He kept saying he was fine, brushing it off like he always did, like the strong Black man he was: one who survived the streets, addiction, and the rest of life in ways most people may not understand. But his face drooped. His footing was uneven, his confusion creeping in.

My mother rushed him out the door and drove him to the hospital, praying under her breath, while I hovered nearby, helpless. My faith shrunk and shook inside my chest. I was a licensed registered nurse with almost a decade of direct patient care on a telemetry and stroke unit; I knew exactly what this looked like and what should be happening medically, and yet in this moment, none of that mattered. My clinical confidence evaporated. This was my father! For the first time in my life, I could not fix what was breaking. When it's the strongest man you know hurting, knowledge suddenly becomes useless.

When they got to the hospital, the nightmare only grew: because of the pandemic, my mom wasn't allowed to stay. She had to hand her husband—this giant of a man we had always depended on physically and spiritually—over to complete strangers. He walked in talking, still himself, and sat alone in the hospital waiting room for hours. Every time we called for an update, my mom's voice would shake. It became obvious my father was deteriorating. His speech was slurring more, his reactions were slower. And then the second stroke hit.

This time it took everything. They rushed him into emergency surgery alone, cutting into his body while none of us could hold his hand, pray over him, whisper encouragement into his ear the way families do.

He lost mobility in his entire right side. He stayed in the hospital for almost a month, alone, isolated, touched by gowns and gloves instead of the people who loved him most. It was soul-crushing. This wasn't just a medical crisis, it was existential.

I felt powerless in a way that split my faith open. I kept asking myself, *How could I not have helped? How could I help strangers, but I couldn't stop this from happening to my own father? Where was God when the strongest man I know was suddenly trapped inside a body that could no longer obey him?*

It confronted me in ways I didn't know were possible, and I could no longer hold everything together. I collapsed—and since I was the strong one, there was no one left to hold me up. The role that had once kept me alive was now killing me. I had been running full speed only to reach the edge of a cliff where there was nowhere to go but off.

I had always been the problem solver, the secret bearer, the person to comfort and carry responsibility for everybody else, and now, I needed help. I needed something tangible to soothe this ache, but life had to go on. Services had to be filmed, the church had to be run, my children had to go to online school, and dinner had to be cooked. Once again, Myesha had to do what she had to do.

You know what I so desperately wanted? I wanted someone to come and see me and say, "No. You go sit down. I will handle this. You need a break! You need to rest. I got it; I will cover you this time." I was ready to run out of gas. I wanted to let it all fall apart. I wanted to choose myself and my health and wellbeing—but I didn't know how. I was afraid of what the unknown would feel like because I had always been in control.

This season was a painful revealer of truth. The truth was not that I was weak, it was that the way I had learned to survive had asked me to move further and further away from myself. I was still functioning, but I was no longer intact. I knew that if I kept living this way, there would be nothing left to recover. My illusion couldn't support me here. Life was getting real, and it was exposing everything that was *not* real. I couldn't avoid it.

Soon after my dad's stroke, before we could catch our breath or make sense of what had happened to him, my younger sister was hospitalized for seizures. Life was coming for us in waves, with no space between the crashes and no time to inhale. One night my mom called me in a panic: my sister had collapsed. She had one seizure, then another, then another, and before my mom could process those, *another* hit. Then a fifth! By the time the paramedics arrived, my sister had suffered almost nine back-to-back seizures with no relief. Her body was betraying her in the most terrifying way. The seizures kept rolling through her like a violent storm she could not escape. My mom tried to explain through tears what was happening, but all I could hear was fear. My stomach tightened and my heart raced. Trauma has a sound, it has a pitch, and I could hear it in my mother's voice.

The paramedics rushed my sister to the same hospital where my dad was recovering from his stroke. When they admitted her, the seizures *still* would not break, so they decided to sedate her and place her into a medically induced coma to give her body a chance to rest. I remember thinking, *Another one, another person I love in crisis, another emergency.* It felt like the entire ground beneath our family was shifting at once.

Having family in two different hospital rooms, between the father who had always been fiercely capable fighting for his mobility and my baby sister who lay unconscious and wrung out from fighting her own body, I felt myself unraveling. I tried to stay strong and compartmentalize, I tried to be the calm, faith-filled daughter everyone expected me to be, but inside I was drowning. I was exhausted in a way that went far beyond physical tiredness; it was spiritual exhaustion, the kind that makes you question everything you believe about life, love, God, and your own capacity to hold pain. I was used to waiting for the other shoe to drop at home, but not everywhere else. Not everywhere at once. I felt useless. Powerless. All the things I once knew and all the confidence I once had did not matter anymore. I had spent a decade caring for other people's families, monitoring strokes, managing medications, and reading vital signs like second nature. Now, when it mattered most, I could not save my own people. Every day when I received updates, my body would tense. What new crisis would I walk into today? What else could possibly go wrong? Yet there I was, holding the weight of all of it while still trying to appear as though I were okay.

This season was not simply hard; it was a deep breaking that reached the bone. Life was stripping me down and pulling apart every illusion that I was in control. It was one of the most confronting periods of my life because it forced me to face the truth that the people I loved were not invincible—and neither was I. I didn't understand, though. I plowed through it. I showed up for my family like I always did. I kept it all together for the church like I always did. I found a strength I didn't know I had, and somehow, I moved through it.

That summer was brutal.

I noticed my middle daughter spending more time in her room. At first, it felt normal. She was in middle school, trying to figure out who she was, navigating hormones and identity and the strange chaos of adolescence. But something inside me knew this isolating was different. It was subtle at first, the way she paused before answering me, the heaviness in her eyes, the quiet that felt too loud. We were all trying to survive the world shutting down, and the walls of our home carried every pressure: the fear of getting sick, the grief of watching my dad fight for his recovery, my sister in a hospital bed, church on a screen. My marriage unraveling. In the middle of all of that, my daughter was slipping into a darkness I could not see clearly yet.

One day I was cleaning her room and opened the closet. There on the wall were words written in ink. Painful words. Words that told the truth before she could tell it out loud. I felt my heart drop. I stood there in that small closet, looking at what she could not say, and I felt the world closing in.

Without panic, I went into mother mode and took her for testing and evaluation immediately. I prayed under my breath in the car even though God felt far at the time, and when the doctors named it depression and anxiety, it felt like someone had turned a light on in a room I had kept dark. At this point, I felt like a failure. I kept asking myself what I had missed, what signs I had not seen. How had I failed to support her? Why was this happening to my family? My daughter was hurting, and I could not save her.

She was put on antidepressants, and I had to fight the shame rising in my chest, the shame that whispered that I should have been able to hold everything together. As if any human being could hold all that life had put on my plate.

In my inner world, God and I were having intense conversations. I felt like I was being asked to carry mountains with bare hands. I wondered why the people I loved most were being hit from every side. What lesson I was supposed to learn? When I would be able to breathe again?

Where does the pastor's wife go to break down? What happens when the woman holding everyone else together finally drops the weight? There was no Sunday service for me to hide behind, no sanctuary to run to, no prayer meeting where someone could lay hands on me and tell me it would all work out. I could not find a place where I felt safe enough to be carried. When I looked around, it seemed like there was no friend to call, no place to safely crumble. My home was full, but I was alone.

I was drowning in plain sight.

So I did what I always did. I kept going. I kept loving. I kept tending to everyone's wounds while my own heart was bleeding out. In September my husband's sister-in-law—a mother, a wife, a daughter, a sister—died of cancer in her thirties. One minute she was fighting, hopeful, surrounded by people who loved her, and the next she was gone. The finality of it struck me in a way I could not articulate. I remember staring at a wall in my house, unable to move, unable to think, wondering how life could be so cruel and so swift.

Her absence spread through the family like a cold front, chilling every room, every conversation, and every plan for the future. Two weeks later, his aunt passed away too. I was tired in a way that went beyond sleep. My spirit felt threadbare. My mind stopped bouncing back. My body felt like it was walking through cement. I kept showing up, kept trying, kept holding everything and everyone, but grief was stacking itself on top of me faster than I could process it. I was unraveling quietly, almost gracefully, the way strong women do when they have been taught their entire lives to break in private. This is what no one tells strong women: strength does not protect you from collapse. It only delays it. And when crash finally comes, it arrives all at once.

What I could not see yet was that this was not a season asking me to endure, it was a season asking me to stop pretending endurance was the same as wholeness.

That entire year broke me down. Layer by layer, piece by piece, blow after blow. My faith was stretched so thin it felt transparent. My capacity as a mother, daughter, sister, and wife was worn to the bone. Every day felt like another reminder that life could change without warning, and every loss carved something out of me that I was not sure I would ever get back. I could feel the edges of my life cracking, spreading, forming fault lines beneath my feet. Even though I kept moving, there was this quiet *knowing* inside of me that the next hit could shatter something I might not be able to put back together.

What came next would not ask me to survive any longer. It would ask me to tell the truth.

THE WEIGHT THAT WASN'T MINE

In early 2021 the world began to reopen. Restrictions were easing and people were hopeful. There was a sense that life might return to something familiar. Inside my home, however, something else was happening.

The day was warm and peaceful. Birds were chirping. It should have been ordinary. Then the phone rang. It was the school nurse. Her tone was calm, professional, and steady, but her words were not. She told me my daughter had said she wanted to harm herself and that I needed to come immediately.

My heart dropped. I prayed the way people pray when language disappears: *God, please. Please.*

I did not ask for understanding; I asked for my child to live. I asked for time. For a moment I felt suspended between disbelief and terror. There is a particular kind of fear that comes with realizing your child is in such deep pain you cannot reach them. I had spent my life believing my attentiveness could prevent they harm, that my vigilance could keep us safe. In that instant, I realized how fragile those beliefs were. I was not facing a problem I could solve. Nothing made sense. She had been on medication for months; she had been seeing a psychiatrist. We had been watching closely, believing we were doing what careful, responsible parents do. I drove to the school in a haze, asking questions the nurse could not answer, my mind searching for a version of this that was less serious than it sounded.

But when I caught sight of my eldest daughter, I knew there was no softer version. Something in her eyes told me this was real, immediate, and dangerous. She told me she wanted help, that she wanted to be admitted somewhere. Hearing my child ask for hospitalization felt surreal, but I listened. I nodded. I explained the process, my voice steadier than I felt, and as soon as we got home, I began calling hospitals.

For a moment she went upstairs. I stayed downstairs on the phone, pacing, waiting, trying to hold the situation together long enough to find a solution. When I walked into her room minutes later, she was sitting in her second story window with her legs dangling outside.

Time slowed. My body reacted before my thoughts did: chest tightened, breath caught. *This is happening. This is actually happening.*

I gently asked her to come inside so we could talk. She listened—she climbed back in, and she cried. Then she said something that shattered whatever sense of orientation I had left: she told me she did not feel safe with me. She said I was part of the problem.

The words pierced me, but I did not argue. I did not correct her. I did not explain myself. I registered the information and focused on what needed to happen next—a familiar instinct. The terror of losing her eclipsed everything else. In moments of crisis, there is little space to deliberate. I knew to assess risk, move toward containment. To act, and to think later.

That night, my daughter asked to attend her school's Bible study. I hesitated, wondering what would stabilize the situation, but I dropped her off and drove away in silence, my hands gripping the steering wheel, my body buzzing with fear.

Around eight o'clock, my phone rang again. It was the youth pastor. He told me my daughter had taken some pills.

I said, "Okay," but my body nearly collapsed in on itself. There are moments when sound disappears and the world narrows to a single point. This was one of them. She had gone to Bible study because she had not died.

I rushed back, picked her up, and drove straight to the emergency room. She was evaluated, tested, and then together we were placed in isolation after she tested positive for Covid.

I sat in that hospital room staring at my child, completely undone, with no sense of how we had arrived there or how we would move forward.

I felt fear, shame, helplessness, and a grief I could not name. I remember looking at her and wishing I could take her pain into my own body if it meant she could be free of it.

The terrifying realization settled in that love does not guarantee safety and effort does not guarantee protection.

When my husband arrived, he came from a different day, a different atmosphere. I felt it immediately. I had already lived through the call, the drive, the intake, and the waiting. I had already crossed the line into something that does not allow you to return unchanged when he walked in from a world that had not yet fractured.

I resented that. The fact that I had been inside the rupture alone. Still, none of that mattered in this room. My world narrowed to the hospital bed, to her face. To the steady rise and fall of her chest. I did not deliberate about whether I should be there; I did not assess my capacity; I did not weigh competing responsibilities. I was her mother. Everything else receded.

The clarity of that was almost violent. There was no confusion about what was mine to carry in that moment. No ambiguity, no negotiation. Just truth.

In the days that followed, once the immediate crisis had slowed and exhaustion had replaced adrenaline, something else began to surface. I realized how different that hospital clarity felt from the way I had been living. Beside her bed, my responsibility had been clean. I knew what belonged to me, what required no justification. Outside of that room, my life had not been so clear.

Carrying what wasn't mine didn't just exhaust me, it trained me. Over time responsibility had started feeling like something I owed others. I had grown accustomed to stepping in before being asked, to absorbing tension before it spread, and to assuming roles because they existed, not because I had chosen them.

In the hospital, though, there was no confusion about choice. I was there because she was my child. That contrast stayed with me.

THE CONVERSATION I WASN'T READY FOR

I didn't go looking for answers. They found me when I was too tired to keep performing. After scrolling on social media one afternoon, a short clip from an episode of an internet show stopped me in my tracks. I remember leaning in, curious, not knowing that what I was about to see would rearrange something inside of me. As soon as I got home, I sat down and pressed play, ready to sink into something deeper. Toward the end of the episode, a psychologist began breaking down relationship dynamics to show how certain patterns form between two people. At the time, I was still holding everything together and drawing closer to the edge than I knew.

At first I watched like a student, taking mental notes, before something shifted. One particular vignette came on, and everything in me went still. I saw myself.

Not the curated version—the First Lady, the strong one. It was *me*, in my most absolute, undeniable form. I watched this woman on the screen respond, comply, over-function, and doubt herself, and with every movement, every flinch, something in me whispered, *This is me*. I felt exposed: seen and terrified all at once, but I kept watching because something in me needed to understand. Was this the language for the ache I could not name? It was like looking into a mirror. My mouth went dry. I had the sense that whatever I was seeing would change how I understood my whole life, and it wasn't just this realization that shook me; it was also the weight lifting off my chest when I understood that I hadn't been failing, I had been adapting. I wasn't broken, I was responding the way someone does when love requires disappearance. For the first time I had a framework. I could lay hold of the pattern I had been circling for years. My shoulders dropped as if my body had been waiting for permission to stop bracing—and my mind went to my husband.

If I could show him this, I thought, maybe he would understand my experience. Maybe we could get help! Maybe what I kept trying to build by myself could be repaired together. Maybe this didn't have to be the ending. As I sat with the significance of what I had just discovered, confusion, self-blame, and more thoughts I had pushed down for years surfaced all at once. I felt comforted and undone at the same time. What I was beginning to understand wasn't who *he* was, but who I had become in the relationship.

That night sleep would not come. My body was exhausted, but my mind stayed awake with the truth. The room was familiar. The body lying inches away from me should have been familiar too, but instead, everything felt foreign. I lay in the dark, staring at the ceiling, breathing through a reality I could not undo. Each inhale and each deep snore from his side of the bed made my body tense. Something had been stripped away; the figure beside me no longer resembled the man I had married. He felt instead like a silhouette I had been devoted to for years, one I could suddenly see clearly, and the clarity was unbearable.

I realized I had spent my adult life loving a version of him that lived mostly in my imagination. I had loved potential. Memory. Hope. I had committed myself to a story I needed to believe to survive, and now I was lying next to evidence that told a different one.

A deep knowing settled into my body, the kind that arrives when you understand life will not return to what it was. I stared at the back of his head and thought, *How did I get here? How did I come to call something love when it caused me so much pain?* In the beginning his attention had felt like devotion. Only later did I wonder how much of what I had experienced was connection and how much was my own longing filling in the gaps. I felt disoriented, as though I had woken up beside someone I did not fully know and was being asked to reckon with what that meant. The fear was quiet and complete.

I lay still, letting the truth land. I had been holding onto an earlier version of him, one I had not seen in years. I had been loving a ghost.

There was no way back. I did not know what would come next, but I knew I could not return to what had been.

The next day I did what I thought was best. In that narrow space between clarity and courage, I made a choice. My hands shook when I reached for my computer—not from fear of him, but from the cost of hoping again. I turned toward him, showed him the video, and said, "I want you to see this. This is how I feel. This is what I have experienced in our relationship." I was offering the last thing I had left: my honesty. It wasn't an ultimatum, but it was my final attempt to stop pretending. "You do not even have to love me," I told him. "Just don't make life hard for me."

I can barely believe I reached that place inside myself where I was willing to accept the absence of love if it meant the pain would stop. At the time I was willing to live without tenderness, warmth, or safety. I just could not tolerate being hurt anymore.

His response was devastating and clarifying at the same time. It made me realized that love cannot survive where truth is treated as a threat. He stopped the video and told me it was dangerous, demonic, and spiritually harmful. There was no pause, no curiosity, no attempt to engage with what I was sharing. I was sitting there with my chest open, offering my truth, and he did not take a single step toward me: not emotionally, not spiritually, and certainly not toward the person I was trying to show him—myself.

For my part, I finally saw not only what he could not offer me, but how much of myself I had set aside in order to stay. Afterward, I sat alone. I wilted in shock, horror, and the realization that the man I loved might be living somewhere I did not have the tools to reach. It felt hauntingly familiar. I had known this helplessness before with my daughter, the aching realization that love alone was not enough to reach someone who was slipping beyond me. Then I whispered to myself, quietly but clearly, "Myesha, what kind of life do you want? Do you want to keep bending until you break? Do you want to keep performing until there is nothing left? Or do you want to move toward something honest and true?"

I had shown my husband that video from a place of both hope and desperation. I had wanted repair, stability, for the life I had built to remain intact even as it was costing me parts of myself. I was afraid of change—but I was just as afraid of staying the same. Something in me was rising. Something steady, something that knew love should not feel like drowning and that survival was no longer enough.

That night something irreversible took root. I did not yet know what I would do, how I would leave, or what it would cost. But after one more truth was spoken and my body understood I would not be met, I could no longer pretend that what I knew would not change how I lived.

Not long after my attempt to be honest with my husband, we were at home meeting with a staff member about the Easter service. We had planned to meet earlier in the day, but my husband had decided to take him to dinner instead. They drank. When they returned, more drinks were poured. Now it was getting late.

I had prepared everything. Agendas printed, timelines mapped, problems identified. I was running the operation, as I often did, but as the night wore on, I only sat at the table listening, tracking where the conversation stalled, watching the same points circle around and around without resolution. Nothing moved forward.

I felt myself withdraw more and more. After an hour or two, I finally said quietly, "I'm going to go to bed. Everything you need is here. You guys can finish up. I am fine with whatever you decide."

The shift was immediate. My husband slammed his hand down, and his voice rose quickly and sharply. He cursed at me loudly, telling me to sit my "fucking ass down" and listen—that we were not done. And then he continued, like nothing had happened.

I felt myself shut down. I had endured that tone before, first in private, then in front of my daughter. This time, there was a new witness—one from outside the family. He had just heard me spoken to in the way I had been spoken to for years . . . and no one did anything to interrupt it.

That moment pierced my soul. It wasn't anything new to me, but this time, I had been exposed. My silence had protected the image of my perfect life right up until now, when it betrayed me.

I went to bed that night and cried myself to sleep. This crossed a line I could no longer excuse. Something irreversible happened within me: once a truth is beheld by witnesses, it can no longer be negotiated away. I knew I would never again be able to pretend I hadn't seen it.

WHEN THE CROWD GREW DISTANT

It took months to re-anchor myself in the truth of my own experience. I was still married, still circulating the same spaces. From the outside, nothing had changed, but inside, everything had.

In quiet conversations behind closed doors, I began telling the truth in fragments, careful sentences offered to a trusted few. I would test the words in the air and watch my friends' faces, searching for confirmation that I was not losing my grip on reality. I was trying to determine whether what I was experiencing was real or whether I had imagined the fracture. I was living in the in-between, known and unknown at the same time.

I told five people my marriage was in trouble. Writing that now feels understated: it was more than "in trouble." It was disintegrating, but I did not yet have language that bold. So I used the softest version available. I said "in trouble" because it was survivable phrasing, because it allowed me to say *something* without yet saying *everything*. Each time I spoke the words aloud, the truth felt both terrifying and stabilizing—like stepping onto thin ice and discovering it would in fact hold.

What I received back was neither confrontation nor rejection, but hesitation. One person told me to go back to him because "you know how Pisces men are." I understood then that what I was naming was destabilizing not just for me, but for others. For the picture to crack meant something familiar could no longer be relied on for any of us.

I tried to extend grace in those early reactions, but it did not erase the loneliness they created. I sat in restaurants crying and saying, "My marriage is not going to make it," while comfort was offered in words rather than presence. Later I became aware that some of these conversations were being repeated elsewhere when I received calls from yet more people encouraging me to hold everything together. Over time I began to hear that some people felt unsure how to engage with me and were choosing to step back. Distance formed through conversations I was not even a part of. Nothing was said directly to me, nothing was explained. I don't know if it was cruelty; it felt more like confusion, other people responding to their own fear of disruption.

We all continued showing up on Sundays and moving through life while I felt increasingly invisible. I was present but no longer oriented. Known, now, but not engaged with. I do not doubt that some people did what they could in the ways they knew how by sending a verse of scripture or reaching out for a brief check-in. Something quieter was being revealed, however: when the role I occupied became uncertain, the relationships attached to it loosened.

For most of my life I had carried the unexamined belief that usefulness created belonging. In this season that belief surfaced clearly. I began to understand that many of the connections I trusted were anchored to function, not intimacy. When my usefulness paused, my proximity to others faded. That clarity did not make me bitter, but it did make me honest. I noticed the absence of others without rushing to interpret it: no calls asking if I was eating, sleeping, or in need of anything, no offers of help. Just space. I had assumed shared history would translate into shared care; I had assumed my showing up for others had built something mutual, but what I began to see instead was that consistency is not the same as closeness. Roles can't sustain connection long after a relationship has thinned.

What stayed with me the most was how rarely anyone asked what was actually happening—until a man from South Africa saw me leaving an event by walking toward my car while my husband headed in another direction. He paused, studied the moment, and later said something did not feel right. "What happened?" he asked.

I told him. He did not redirect me, and he did not try to stabilize the moment. He simply listened, and his question clarified something essential for me: presence does not require certainty. It only requires willingness to listen.

This whole season taught me how to stop outsourcing my understanding of my own life, how to listen to my own voice without waiting for reinforcement, how to recognize the difference between being valued for what I carried and being known for who I am. I learned that a role can create access, but it cannot guarantee care. When people talk about the unraveling of a marriage, they often focus on the obvious, but beneath it are subtler losses. Familiar rhythms, assumed belonging, social certainty. For me, this chapter was not only about the marriage ending. It was also about releasing the belief that usefulness ensured connection.

I understood what was happening at this point, but I did not expect it to arrive so quietly. What I did not realize then was that my clarity would soon require action; simply knowing the truth would no longer be enough. There would come a moment when I would be asked to preserve comfort at the expense of honesty, and for the first time in my life, I would not.

THE FIRST TIME I DIDN'T COMPLY

I had spent most of my life believing that endurance was love, that staying was virtue, that my ability to absorb pain without complaint was evidence of spiritual maturity—but there comes a moment when the body reaches a truth the mind can no longer negotiate away. Once I saw it, compliance was no longer possible.

The unraveling did not happen loudly. It happened in whispers, in private confessions, in the quiet hope that if I told the truth carefully enough, someone would meet me there. There were things happening behind the scenes that I could no longer ignore; the pressure at the church had increased far beyond my mere workload, which in and of itself was enormous, to more than the weight of ministry or leadership. I was being triangulated in ways that felt unfair. A new woman entered the environment in a way that I experienced as comparison and diminishment. Within days of my stepping away, someone else was working from my office, and the timing landed in my body as replacement. There were conversations I was not part of, decisions being made without my voice, and an energy that made it clear that a door was quietly, deliberately closing behind me. I was being edged out.

Before my husband and I ever made the decision to part ways, I fought with everything in me to preserve what we had. I gave every ounce of hope and logic and love I could think of, but I had experienced so many losses by then that I was emptied out. I had run out of gas inside myself; I could no longer be the engine, the one making everything happen. I had no strength left. I needed care, reciprocity, and partnership, the basic conditions of a shared life. Yet because I had allowed my marriage to run the way it did for so many years, it became impossible to renegotiate anything else. We could not simply sit down and say, "Here is what you have been doing, here is what I have been doing, and here is what we need to change." That conversation was not happening in any real way. I was reaching the point where I had to make the hardest decision. I could no longer be present in a marriage where I was not receiving what every human being deserves.

But the first thing I had to release was the church.

I thought I was choosing health and rest, but what I did not yet see was that this was the first time I was choosing *myself* without asking permission. At first I assumed I was overwhelmed simply because I had taken on too much responsibility. I was doing the job of four or five people: leading, singing, hiring, firing, running operations and supporting every ministry I could. I was honoring God, honoring my children, honoring the work, and trying to be everything my husband wanted and expected. By now I had reached a point where I thought, *I am going to die if something does not change. Something is so fundamentally broken here that I will not survive it.* I could feel it in my bones. That was the truth. Leave or die.

I went to my husband with love in my heart and said I could not do the church part anymore. I would rather step away, let him find someone else, and focus on being a wife and a mother. I wanted to speak, to sing, to create on my own—just to live. Maybe we did not *need* to work together. Maybe we needed to protect the marriage instead of sacrificing it on the altar of ministry.

But in the traditional Christian house, the man is the head. His voice overrides the wife's. In our home my husband was the leader, and at church he was my boss. In ministry he was my pastor. In daily life he was my husband and the father of my children. There was not one slice of my life where he was not present, influencing decisions whether he was physically there or not. Slowly I had realized there was nowhere in that pie where Myesha existed for herself. I believed that if I could just release the church part, if I could lift that weight off my shoulders and off of my chest, maybe we could save our relationship. If I could remove the pressure on me, maybe we could both breathe again. I thought, *Let me let go of every-thing else. I do not have to speak. I do not have to sing. I do not have to show up for every ministry moment. I do not have to work there. Let me rest. Let me breathe. Let us focus on us.*

But this was not accepted.

There was no room for negotiating. No space for compromise. That was the moment I understood another truth I had been avoiding: this was not a partnership strained by circumstance, it was a system that required my compliance to survive. Once I stopped complying, it had no interest in keeping me.

My husband was not a typical boss. From the beginning I was taught that when words came out of his mouth, I should have a pen in my hand, and nothing less than perfection seemed acceptable. We would work late into the night on projects, flyers, graphics, presentations. Hours of labor and careful execution, and if he walked in the next morning and saw a single mistake, everything went into the trash. The entire project. The time, the effort—gone. And his displeasure was not handled privately. He expressed it openly, in front of whatever staff were present, and his praise was rare. The pressure on me was constant. He would speak in circles about what he wanted, give directives, and then forget what he had said. There was no follow-up. His expectations shifted without warning, and somehow it was always my responsibility to translate his vision, interpret his moods, anticipate his needs, and make everything happen anyway with excellence, with speed, and without question. I learned how to read his mind before he finished speaking, how to protect the team by absorb-ing the pressure myself. I was the filter, the fixer, the one who made sure nothing fell apart.

It was an environment that demanded constant vigilance. People other than me burned out; turnover was high. Many ended up in therapy after they left. I managed to endure because I lived with him; I was used to it. I knew how to calm him down, how to redirect his focus, how to keep things moving.

I told myself this was my strength. I had worked in high pressure envi-ronments before—I had been a nurse for almost ten years. I had multiple degrees, including two master's. I had handled life and death and navigated chaos. I believed my ability to manage difficult people was a superpower.

But I paid for it.

Working with my husband was not collaborative leadership. There was no coming alongside, no shared load. It was always "whatever it takes, make it happen," and if it did not happen, the consequences for me were clear. I carried the weight of execution while he carried the authority. I took the notes, shaped the ideas, built the systems, and then handed them over so they could be spoken through someone else's voice.

For a long time that was acceptable to me. I told myself it was service, said it was humility, part of the calling. I was in the background making everything work while he stood in the spotlight receiving the credit. That arrangement worked until it didn't. It was not that I wanted less work; I wanted dignity. I wanted to be valued, honored, to be seen as the professional woman I was. And I wanted safety, emotional regulation, and a working environment where excellence did not require fear. Where my ideas did not have to be filtered through someone else to be legitimate. This was not simply about exhaustion, it was about self-worth. It was about realizing that the pressure I was under was not sustainable because the cost was my integrity. I needed a lifeline, and I knew it could not be found inside a system that required me to disappear in order for it to function.

I made a decision. At the end of the year—on December 31—I was out. I was done. I had reached the point where I was either going to die working there, or I was going to walk away and figure out what came next. Those were the only two roads left.

My husband did not understand. He wanted to keep talking it through, but I had already explained. I had pleaded. I had tried to make him see what was happening to me. No one was hearing me. I knew that if I did not choose myself in that moment, there would be no return. I was losing pieces of myself faster than I could recover them.

We had one last staff meeting. In the middle of it, I spoke. I said that I loved the work we had all done together. I thanked everyone for everything we had built. This had been the only church I had ever been part of in my entire life; I had grown up in this ministry. I had loved serving the people, carrying the vision, and using every gift I had to help people and talk to them about God. It was meaningful to me, sacred. It shaped me.

Then I said that starting next year, I would no longer be working on staff. I told them I would remain a member of the church, but I needed time. Time for my family, time for myself, time to breathe. Time to understand what was happening inside my life.

The response was meek. Muted. Almost as if they did not quite know what to say. I remember someone whispering, "Are they going to get a divorce?" I sat there thinking, *What are they talking about?* I was not quitting my marriage, I was quitting a job. I simply could not work there anymore. It was too much pressure, too heavy, too consuming. I needed space to be human, to find my footing, to understand what was happening within my own soul. My body had already crossed a line my mouth was only just catching up to.

But that person was right about one thing: leaving the church did not save my marriage. It exposed it. I was not actively dismantling our life, but I *was* stepping out of the role that had been the only thing holding it together. And once I did, there was nothing left to hide behind.

After I stepped away from service at the church, the atmosphere changed quickly. The distance I felt between myself and other congregants was immediate and unmistakable. What I had hoped would create space for me to breathe in peace instead created an atmosphere of suspicion. What I believed might protect the marriage instead destabilized the whole structure. My refusal to keep absorbing the weight of everything had shifted the balance, and when a system senses that it is losing control, it tightens.

Not long after this I was traveling with my husband and children and staying at a local hotel. The details of the trip matter less than what happened inside that room. That night, while I slept, he went through my phone.

He scrolled through my direct messages, reviewing a group chat between me, my mother, and my sisters. It was ordinary, familiar, full of family language. There were videos and memes that referenced breakups and relationships sent by my sister about something she was navigating in her own life. Nothing about me, though. Nothing secret, nothing I was trying to hide.

But at three in the morning, he woke me up.

He did not tell me what he had done. He began asking questions instead. Calm at first, then more pointed. Then circular. I was disoriented, half asleep, confused about what he was even referring to. Every answer I gave seemed to provoke another question. I did not know that he had screenshots. I did not know that he was building a case.

The questioning continued for hours.

I remember the sun starting to rise and realizing that I had not had much sleep at all. My body was rigid. My chest felt tight. I was afraid, though I did not yet know why. Eventually he told me to call my family— my mother, my sisters. He told me to ask them to come to our house, but not to tell them why.

That instruction signaled danger in my body.

My family does not move lightly, but they protect fiercely. They do not tolerate harm. I knew that if I told them I was scared or in trouble, the situation would escalate in ways no one could control. So I did exactly what he asked. I called them and said only that I needed them to come over.

They came immediately.

When we arrived home from the hotel, they were already there. Their faces were concerned, confused. They thought something terrible had happened to me physically—illness, emergency. They did not know what they were walking into.

He asked for my mother and sisters to sit down, and then he began questioning them. He asked what I had told them, asked them what they knew, why they were sending me videos. He implied interference, manipulation with intent. My family members looked at one another, bewildered. They told him they did not know what he was talking about, but they explained the group chat. They answered calmly.

I sat there silent. I was terrified; I could feel my heart in my throat. My hands were cold. My body knew something my mind was still trying to catch up to: this was no longer a private dynamic. This was exposure.

Later, my family told me they had never seen fear like that in my eyes. They said that something unspeakable must be wrong for me to look the way I did.

Eventually the confrontation escalated. Voices were getting louder, defensiveness was kicking it while I prayed with my entire heart. And then the arguing dissipated. There was no resolution, no apology, and no clarity. My family left, shaken. Polite. Watchful.

Something irreversible had happened. The rabbit was out of the hole.

This was the moment the whole system cracked open. It was the first time my family saw what I had been managing alone. The story could no longer be contained by my silence.

After that nothing returned to normal. There was no repair conversation, no regrouping, no rebuilding. The air between me and my husband changed. Safety did not slowly erode this time; it disappeared entirely. I did not yet call it the end, but my body knew. This was not conflict. This was control reacting to loss. I understood, finally, with a clarity that left no room for negotiation, that the moment I stopped complying, the structure that depended on my compliance had revealed itself completely.

It was downhill after that. Everything that followed did not break the marriage, it only made visible what had already been true for a long time.

WHEN SAFETY DISAPPEARED

We started the new year pretending everything was fine. On the outside it looked manageable. We were still in the same house, still moving through familiar routines, still performing the roles we had memorized for seventeen years—but I felt a distance, a coldness between us that no amount of smiling, Sunday service, or marital duty could soften. By then I had done too much reading, too much studying, too much listening to people who understood the psychological terrain I was living in. I was educating myself quietly, trying to understand the dynamics of my life and thinking about survival.

I had non-negotiables now, real ones. Ones rooted in basic human dignity. I needed to be treated as a person with inherent value, not as a supply of labor, service, sex, or emotional availability that flowed in only one direction. I was not asking for perfection. I needed the *bare minimum*: Care. Accountability. Space to breathe. Partnership in parenting rather than carrying the full weight alone. I had carried most of everything for years without complaint. I was simply refusing to carry more than I could survive.

I drew a line. I said that for the marriage to continue, things had to change. We needed couple's therapy, real support, real help.

My husband agreed. As therapy went on, however, I experienced his participation as guarded and inconsistent. What I shared in session resurfaced at home in ways that left me feeling exposed rather than protected. Our sessions continued for several weeks. At one point, the therapist looked at me and said quietly that she was not sure I would get what I wanted out of it. I understood exactly what she meant.

I told him we should stop. The truth was already free to see. Continuing felt like prolonging something that was no longer viable. But instead of relief, I felt more cautious. There had been no repair, and now I felt watched.

Around that time the dynamic between us shifted again: I felt discarded. That is the only word for it. His attention moved elsewhere, and his loyalty felt less certain. Small moments accumulated. Nothing dramatic on its own, but it was unmistakable in its pattern. The mask slipped from his face more often, and the ground beneath me felt treacherous. I was afraid. More than afraid—I began to feel unsafe in ways I could not dismiss. I began drafting letters and having them notarized, documenting that I was of sound mind, because I did not know what might be said about me or done in response to the boundaries I was setting. That is how fragile my inner world had become.

Even now I kept telling myself that if I could just get through one more week, something might shift. But a deeper truth was rising in me. There were several moments on the road to the end, but one changed everything.

By now my husband would reference conversations in ways that unsettled me, as though my space no longer belonged to me. Phrases surfaced that I had spoken only to my family, and other small clues appeared. His comments landed with too much familiarity. It felt like something I had believed was private was no longer privileged information.

I grew quieter in the house, stopped speaking openly. Phone calls happened outside while I walked the neighborhood, sat in the backyard, or paced the street. And my voice changed. After years of restraint, I began speaking honestly to my family for the first time. Sometimes that honesty came out raw, even profanely, shaped by how much pain I had been holding. But it was the first time my truth had existed without careful editing.

I knew something was not right. I believed my privacy was being compromised even though I did not yet have proof. I tore my car apart. It was a brand-new Mercedes SUV, the first car I had ever purchased entirely in my own name, one I'd chosen and financed myself. It symbolized agency, awakening, a woman coming back to life—and now I was searching it in fear. Under the seats, inside panels, in the trunk. I found nothing, and the absence of evidence made the fear worse, not better.

I went to a specialty electronics store and asked for a scan. Their device reacted strongly in one area of the car, but no visible equipment was found. That ambiguity intensified my vigilance. I could not see what I feared. I could not touch it, could not prove it. So I confronted my husband. I asked why. I said it was not okay. He denied it repeatedly, but eventually, during one of these confrontations, he acknowledged that my conversations had been recorded. My husband showed me a recording device that amounted to seventeen hours of material. Private moments, private pain—conversations I had *never* consented to being preserved. There was no explanation that restored a sense of safety for me.

I also noticed unusual activity on my digital accounts that I could not explain at the time: messages read before I saw them, settings changed. My sense of security deteriorated. By then my body was no longer guessing, it was responding to what I perceived as danger, my nervous system shifting into constant alert. I did the only thing I knew to do.

New passwords. New email. New phone. New devices.

I sold my car because I could not sit inside it without feeling watched. What once symbolized freedom now symbolized fear. I created a code word with my family so they would know if I was in trouble. I lived in a state of vigilance that never fully shut off. And when he finally acknowledged what I believed had been happening, something in my heart closed for good.

There was no more talking.

No more repairing.

No more hoping.

Something inside me signed its own papers.

That was the moment I knew the marriage was over. The question was no longer whether I could stay, it was whether I could survive if I did.

Boundaries are not ultimatums. They are the place where self-abandonment ends.

That was the moment I chose myself.

TELLING THE CHILDREN THE TRUTH

Nothing mattered more to me than how this would land on my children. I love them more than anything in this world; being their mother has always been the most meaningful and sacred role of my life. It's anchored me, it's steadied me, it has given me purpose when everything else felt unstable. I poured myself into creating a life that felt safe for them. I showed up for every need, every moment, every milestone.

Because of that, I wanted to speak to them without my husband con-trolling the narrative, the timing, or the framing. I needed the truth to come from me, but I was terrified. My body knew what I was about to do before my mind could fully catch up: my husband did not want me to tell them. In choosing to speak in my own voice, I would defy him. But I was choosing my children over that perfect image I had spent so many years protecting. Now I was choosing honesty over performance. I was choosing my voice over my fear.

When it came time to sit them down and tell them that we were divorcing, I understood that the moment would stay with them; it would become part of the story they carried forward. That truth did not make the decision easier, but it made it clearer. I had to accept yet another painful truth—that my decision, no matter how necessary, might one day be part of the reason they walk into a therapist's office. Acknowledging that gave me clarity. However, based on what they had already seen and felt growing up, they were going to need support whether I stayed or left. They were already carrying things that required care.

If their future need for healing was inevitable, I wanted it rooted in truth rather than the preservation of a fantasy. I wanted them to grow up knowing that life can break open and still lead somewhere good, that choosing yourself is not betrayal, but integrity. That courage sometimes means telling the harder truth now so that real healing can come later.

I started one child at a time.

I sat with them individually, my hands shaking so badly I kept them folded in my lap, my heart beating fast and loud in my chest. Their eyes are something I will never forget. I saw confusion. I saw disappointment. I also saw something that looked like recognition. Children often sense truth long before adults are brave enough to speak it.

They needed to hear what every child needs to hear in moments like this: You are loved. You are safe. You are going to be okay. I told them they had two parents who loved them, even as the marriage ended. That their lives were not breaking, only changing shape. That none of this was their fault. That their world was not disappearing, only becoming something new.

Mothers are conditioned to sacrifice themselves for their children. We love our children more than our own breath. I knew I had a choice. I could choose immediate comfort, or I could choose truth and allow my children the chance to build healthier lives in the long run. Staying silent would teach them to silence themselves, and pretending everything was all right would teach them to tolerate dysfunction because it felt familiar. I could not do that. Not to them. Not anymore.

What I understood in that moment was this: telling the children the truth was not about disclosure so much as it was about alignment. I could no longer ask my body to live inside a lie, even in the name of protection. I had to choose honesty if any of us were to reach safety.

After I spoke to them individually, later that night, we gathered as a family, my husband included, and walked through the truth together.

We cried. We tried to make sense of something that did not fully make sense.

This was the defining moment of my motherhood. It was the moment I stopped modeling endurance and started modeling integrity.

THE DAY THE HOUSE WENT QUIET

After that conversation everything happened so quickly it almost felt intentional. On the first weekend of April my husband moved out. Every other time we had transitioned between homes, I had been the one who packed the boxes, hired the movers. My family helped me as needed, but he was rarely involved. Now, when it was time to leave, he moved out first, all by himself.

I walked into the house, went straight to the closet, and every single one of his things was gone. The moment felt surreal. Empty rods, a few hangers still swinging back and forth. A strange emptiness in the air. A handful of stray items remained, but his absence was loud, creating a hollow feeling in the room—a confirmation of everything that had been unraveling inside of me long before this day.

We were no longer together. Our marriage was over.

I wish I could say I felt only relief in that moment. In some ways I did. The pressure lifted in places where it had been crushing me for years. There was no one to anticipate or manage, no more tension waiting to explode, no argument hovering just beneath the surface. The house felt slower, the air felt different, the silence was the first silence in years that did not terrify me. But I would be lying if I said I did not feel sadness too.

I felt many things at once: lost, hurt, and the quiet grief of asking myself how we ended up here. Relief and sorrow occupied the same space in my body. There was freedom, but there was also a vacant place where something familiar used to live. A void. Endings, even necessary ones, still ask you to mourn what you hoped might have been.

Lastly, beneath all of it, fear began to surface. The fear of the unknown. *How can I be alone?*

What will life look like now?

Who am I without the role I have performed for nearly two decades?

The kids still had their rooms and their rhythms, and I still had responsibilities. I had always done almost everything anyway, so the day-to-day tasks didn't feel unfamiliar. But something inside me was shaking itself awake. The truth was, I had become deeply codependent. I had been conditioned to need to feel needed and had shaped myself around being the person who held everything together. That dysfunction was painful, but it was familiar, and the dysfunction you know often feels safer than the unknown you are walking toward.

What made that day even more disorienting was that I hadn't been home when he left; I only walked into the aftermath. I didn't see him pack, I didn't see him close the door for the last time. I only saw the results. For years, I had been told he couldn't do these things, but in one weekend, he did all of them. I had been made to believe he didn't know how. All that time, he could have. He simply hadn't.

A heaviness settled in my chest when I realized my life had been shaped around a narrative that was never true. The quiet in the house was strange and heavy. It was the quiet of truth.

Then something else became unmistakably clear: his physical absence finally matched the emotional absence I had lived with for years. The empty closet revealed what I had known all along—even when his clothes were there, I had been alone. Even when the house was full, I had been alone. I had been carrying the weight of the marriage by myself.

He had never really been home.

I finally saw clearly that my emotional and physical realities were aligning. The life I had been performing was ending, and the life I had been avoiding was beginning to take shape.

✳✳✳

My husband and I met with a mediator to begin the formal process of divorce. I knew I was stepping into a new reality, but what I did not yet understand was how little control I would have over how this ending would unfold. In the weeks after he moved out, I had moved slowly. I was still orienting myself inside the quiet, still learning how to breathe in a life that no longer required constant vigilance. I was focused on stabilizing myself, not realizing how quickly the ground beneath me was about to shift.

That Sunday, although I was invited to church for prayer, I could not step foot into that building. My body would not move in that direction; my spirit would not let me go. I had spent nearly two decades forcing myself to show up in spaces that were breaking me to perform strength I did not have, two decades holding together a life collapsing from the inside. After everything had been shared without my consent, something in me finally said no.

So I stayed home. I stayed in the quiet. I stayed with myself. And the silence from everyone else after I missed church spoke louder than any sermon ever had.

The narrative for my absence was shaped by whatever people needed to believe to protect themselves. Rumors spread quickly, anchored by the official statement that there had been no abuse and no infidelity. My phone buzzed nonstop. *Are you okay? What happened? I'm so sorry.* But beneath the questions, I could feel the tremble of people seeking reassurance more than truth. For years I had been upheld by their approval of my service, of the identity I had built inside that church. In a single moment all of that was stripped away.

Choosing myself felt like betraying an entire community, yet it was the only chance I had left to save my own soul. I didn't know how I would make it. I didn't know what life would look like on the other side of this unraveling. All I knew was that something had ended in me and something else had begun. But I had poured everything into that church. I had sacrificed years with my children, my family, my ambitions, and most of all, my voice. I had molded myself into the version of me that they needed and praised. When it all collapsed, I could only stand in the wreckage asking who I was without the illusion, without the applause, and without the narrative I had built just to survive.

Missing church that Sunday wasn't a conscious decision; it was my spirit refusing to betray itself one more time. It was yet more truth rising before I was ready to speak it. This collapse broke me into tiny pieces, but it also revealed everything else that had been breaking me all along. In that raw quiet, I finally faced the truth I had been circling for years: I had always known there was a life meant for me beyond the performance, beyond the spotless reputation, beyond the four walls that defined my worth. What I hadn't known was how to live that life and remain who the world expected me to be. It was impossible.

Instead, somewhere along the way had I decided the only way to preserve the marriage was to surrender myself—at that time, preserving the marriage was paramount to me. I trained myself to accept breadcrumbs and call it blessing, letting the world believe I was fulfilled while I was starving inside. So when I stopped performing, when I stopped contorting myself to survive, I was left with the question I had avoided my entire life: *Who am I when I am no longer pretending?*

I had spent my life becoming who others needed. But now, I needed myself. It was time to meet her.

BROKEN IN FULL VIEW

My husband had hit "send" on a few thousand characters and turned my private life into public property. The shift in my body as I watched it all unfold happened beneath thought: my chest locked, and my hands shook. These would be no going back to who I had been an hour earlier.

After I screamed my lungs out, crying until there were no tears left, hopelessness arrived in my heart. *Why try?* I couldn't stay, couldn't go, couldn't stand, couldn't pray—couldn't fix it. I remember sitting on the edge of my bed, phone in my hand, staring at messages I didn't know how to answer. The room was quiet in a way that felt hostile. I realized I hadn't eaten all day, but even that felt irrelevant. The life I had been standing in no longer existed.

In the days that followed, I walked to metabolize the anxiety and move grief through my body. I averaged thirty-two thousand steps a day. My feet kept moving because my thoughts would not stop; my body was processing what my mind could not hold. The temptation was to suppress the emotion, to bury it, to pretend this had not happened. I wanted to hide from the magnitude of it, to skip ahead to some future version of myself who had survived, but there was no way around it. Only through.

I was not prepared to survive this kind of trauma publicly. I had been protected by the image of perfection, but when it cracked, it became a cage. Once the truth was known, there was nowhere left to hide. I was a pastoral leader—I loved the church, I loved the people, I loved what we had built. And still, my life was falling apart, and there was no one to rescue me. I had carried so many through their hardest moments, I had known what to say when everything fell apart for them, but when it was my turn, there was no altar to run to. No spiritual tribe to catch me. Just silence.

That silence did something to me. I kept asking how this could be happening, after all I had done to serve God, to serve His people, to do it right. My situation felt unjust. I wish I could say a prayer partner came to me during this time or a pastor spoke over me, that the people I poured into poured back into me. But they didn't. I kept thinking of the middle-school version of myself who just wanted to be loved and accepted. I cried for her. I cried for her sense of abandonment, for the perfect life I had built for her on the outside, hoping one day it would feel real, only for it to be detonated and leave me sitting in the debris.

The version of me who could keep pretending died there. Nothing would ever be the same.

My turning point came from one decision. No rescue arrived, no voice spoke over me. There was only a choice: stay, or disappear. And I chose to stay in my body.

Choosing to stay did not feel brave. It felt mechanical. I made the smallest decisions possible: Breathe again. Stand up. Drink water. Stay alive. I was not choosing a future yet; I was simply choosing not to vanish. But that choice shifted something.

I began thinking about the woman I might become if I survived this, the woman who would learn how to walk through it. This moment right here was not the whole story. It was one chapter. There could be others if I kept going. Besides, there weren't many options left. It was either move through this moment or remain buried inside it forever.

So I started. Slowly. Imperfectly. I had to heal pain that existed long before my marriage. I had to confront parts of myself I had kept hidden my whole life, and avoidance had only delayed the reckoning. Isolation had only deepened the wound. It's easier to put trauma in a drawer and pretend it doesn't exist; everything in me still wanted to hide. But something stronger said *no*. I would walk toward what hurt. I would stop running from the truth.

The end of my marriage was not my funeral, but it was the death of the life I had been protecting. Choosing truth did not bring relief, it brought exposure, and while the collapse may not have destroyed me, it did end the version of myself built on performance.

Here, for the first time, I understood that survival would require more than endurance. It would require *me*.

LOSS OF LANGUAGE

WHEN BELIEFS STOPPED WORKING

My every attempt to move forward was met with resistance from others, visible and invisible. I was still showing up for my children, still doing the ordinary things that anchor a life; for the most part, I looked functional, but inside, I was unmoored. One afternoon, sitting in the pickup line outside my youngest daughter's school, I was on the phone with my mom and my sisters. Something had happened again—another threat. Another reminder that even after the divorce, my former husband's control had not fully ended.

As I spoke with my family, something inside me slipped out of alignment. I started crying and said, "I'm never going to get beyond this. Why would God allow me to suffer like this?" Then I said the thing that frightened me: "Maybe death is the only way."

I did not want to die, but I had to name the depth of the pain. I didn't have any other language for it. I wanted the pressure to release, the noise to stop.

I pulled myself back even as the words hung between myself and my family members. *You do not need to die to solve this. You must keep walking,* I told myself. But the moment mattered; it revealed how lost I felt inside my own life. I was angry with God! I had given my life to faith, to service, to doing things the right way. I'd believed in the promise I'd been told. Now I was driving down the street, staring at green grass and trees, shouting questions into the air that had no place to land: "Why would You allow this? How does any of this glorify You? This is not victory."

What I was experiencing was the loss of orientation: the beliefs that had once told me who I was, where I stood, and how to decide no longer worked. I did not know how to locate myself in the world anymore. For the first time in my life, I now understood the people who walk away from God after unbearable loss—I understood it viscerally. I had entered the terrain where belief stops functioning as a compass, where the language that once steadied you no longer points anywhere. It was not just that my marriage had ended; the entire framework I had used to make sense of my life had collapsed.

I watched from the outside as life continued without me. The friends, routines, church, and the roles remained with my former husband. The only thing that was replaced was me.

This, even after everything else, was my dark night of the soul. God didn't disappear, but the structure I used to reach Him did. It happened quickly; I went to bed one person and woke up without a map. All I had left to go on was myself—and the version of me who knew how to function inside a church world was gone, replaced by another version I had never met before. The one who would have to move forward without everything I'd known before.

When my beliefs stopped working, it was disorienting. The rules I had used to navigate my life no longer applied, and I did not yet have replacements for them. I could feel myself searching for something solid enough to hold me, but I did not know where to look. In the days that followed, I didn't need theology; I needed orientation, something that could tell me where I was and how to move without betraying myself.

Many of us do not realize how much our beliefs are doing for us until they stop telling us where we are. There is nothing more destabilizing than that kind of disorientation. I needed to find my center again, my anchor, my sense of direction. For the first time in my life, I did not know where to look.

WHEN I NEEDED AIR

My sister saw the condition I was in. Anxiety about my future had taken me over, and I was flooded with questions: Who would I become? Where would I land? Was I making the right choice? She looked at me then and said, "Myesha, I think you should consult."

"Consult with what?" I asked, feeling desperate. Prayer and devotions no longer soothed me, and therapy felt too slow for the unbearable level of pain I was carrying. I was looking for something to steady my body long enough to breathe again. But when she said, "You should consult a psychic," it stopped me cold.

The religious framework I had been raised in was not working for me in that moment, but this felt forbidden. Yet my sister told me she had spoken to this woman before, that she was kind, that it might help. I remember sneaking around as I took her advice; I was terrified someone would find out. I got the phone number and tried to pay in a way that would not leave a trail. *That* is how trained I was to think about perception, about how anything could be misinterpreted or used against me. I wasn't afraid of what the psychic might say, I was afraid of crossing a line I had been taught never to question.

But I had spent my whole life obeying rules that had never been tested by real crisis. Pain has a way of exposing what is performative. I wasn't rebellious; I was reaching for relief. When the nervous system is overwhelmed, it looks for signals of safety. That is what I was searching for.

I made the appointment and then forced myself to push it out of my mind so I wouldn't spiral and cancel it. Fear lived in my body—but so did hope. Desperation. A quiet plea for clarity I could not find anywhere else.

When the day of the call came, I was able to remain functional. I showed up for my children, moved through the motions of my life as the hours passed, though much of my actual life now felt unfamiliar. As for my future, it had become a blank space; the plans I had once held tightly for the next ten years, even the next six months, had evaporated. My entire nervous system felt like it was trembling while I waited for the time to call even though my body was still.

When the psychic answered the phone, her voice was warm. Calm. Settled. My sister and I affectionately came to refer to her as Aunt Cynthia because the comfort in her tone felt familiar, like the embodiment of a relative we had lost. It felt like grace reaching toward me in a way I was not used to receiving. Aunt Cynthia did not tell me the future or make decisions for me. It wasn't about hearing some dramatic storyline; she simply met me where I was. Whether it was spiritual, psychological, or merely the steadiness of her presence, her effect on my body was real. She confirmed what I already knew deep in my gut: I would be okay, and the shift I was sensing inside myself was real. I was not imagining it. Her voice steadied me.

That first call led to several more, especially during the most heightened moments of my separation. But I felt guilty. I had been trained to believe comfort had to come through approved channels, conditioned to distrust my own knowing. Trauma, however, makes a person reach for anything that feels like breath, and I was suffocating. I was receiving threatening messages, dealing with unpredictable reactions, and through it all trying to keep myself from being pulled under. Whenever I needed reinforcement, whenever I needed to remember that my intuition was not lying to me, I would call Aunt Cynthia. Every time, she met me with peace. Never fear, never manipulation, just clarity.

At some point she disappeared. She left the psychic service entirely, and I found no trace of her again. But I understood that our time was complete. She had been there for a specific season, solely to point me back to myself. To remind me that I hear well and see well, and that everything I needed to move forward was already within me. Truthfully, it mirrored the part of church I had once relied on, the ability to go to someone and say, "I am hurting. Can you pray for me?" Except this time, I was not seeking a prophetic word. I was seeking air. I needed one sign that I would not drown.

And strangely, through the words of Aunt Cynthia, I learned I did not need to seek outward signs anymore at all. My guidance had been within me all along.

Sometimes the thing that steadies us does not arrive through the structures we were taught to trust. Sometimes it arrives as permission to look elsewhere for confirmation that what we feared we had lost was never gone at all.

THE QUIET BETWEEN

There are moments in life when choosing yourself costs you almost every-thing. It may not happen all once, but piece by piece, certainty goes first, then reputation, then the familiar language you used to explain yourself to the world. It rearranges the interior of your life in ways you cannot rush. I realized I could no longer survive by explaining myself before I understood who I was becoming.

I decided that before I close my eyes for the last time on this earth, I wanted at least one chapter of my life to tell the truth. A *lived* chapter. I wanted to know, in my bones, that love did not require bruising, that respect did not require smallness, and that devotion did not require disappearance. I wanted to know that my humanity was not something I had to barter away in order to be held. So, for the first time in years, I began talking to God without a script. I spoke to the God who sees beneath language, the God who hears the prayers we do not yet have words for, and in one of the most exposed moments of my life, I said what I had been afraid to admit even to myself: If choosing myself meant I would not have all the answers, I would accept it.

If it meant walking forward without being understood, I accepted that too. If it required releasing the certainty I had once clung to, I was willing. I could no longer continue in a life that required me to betray myself in order to preserve it.

What followed was the strange stillness that comes after a structure dissolves but before a new one forms. I had released the life I knew, but I had not yet learned how to live without it. Relinquishing the silence that could no longer protect me left me without language. It exposed how little vocabulary I had for my own needs, which I felt deeply—urgently. But I did not yet know how to translate these needs into choices, boundaries, or direction. I could sense truth in my body, but I couldn't articulate it with confidence. It was as though my internal operating system was in the middle of an update, and everything familiar had gone offline. The instincts I once trusted no longer applied. I was still breathing, still moving through my days, but I was not fully functional while something new was installing.

I had spent so much of my life orienting myself through roles, expectations, and service. Without those frameworks, I did not know where to stand. I did not know how to make decisions without bracing for consequence or approval. I did not know how to exist without earning my place.

The stillness became a kind of wilderness. Exposing, sacred and frightening at the same time. It was holy ground without markers. Here, I no longer had to explain myself to anyone; I could learn how to listen to myself.

I was not yet ready to rebuild meaning. First I had to learn how to live without it, how to stay present in the space between what had fallen apart and what had not yet arrived. How to trust that understanding would return in its own time. This was a season of honesty. I stopped pretending I knew what came next, I stopped narrating my pain into something acceptable. I let myself stand without armor, without explanation, and without resolution.

And slowly, something unexpected happened.

I realized I was still held.

Without certainty or structure, I was held by presence.

The rediscovery began with permission. Permission to exist without proving. Permission to feel without translating. Permission to live inside the question.

In that quiet between frameworks, I discovered that God had not been waiting for me to understand. God had been waiting for me to stop hiding.

THE ART OF LETTING GO

I tried going no contact with my former husband for a couple of months, and I failed at it.

I had never gone a day without speaking to the person I had built my entire adult life with, and suddenly I was expected to cut him off completely. Something in me resisted. This did not feel like alignment, it felt like force, like I was being asked to become a version of myself I was not ready to inhabit yet. Friends, therapists, and well-meaning voices all had opinions about what I should do. They spoke with certainty, but none of it settled in my spirit. Ignoring his calls felt mean, and not responding felt cruel. I was not built for hostility or erasure—even directed toward him. Even in the middle of everything, I still cared. That was my truth.

By the middle of the summer, a few months after the public announcement of our separation in May, the weight of it all was wearing me down. My former husband had been out of the country, and when he returned, he drove straight to my house to see the kids. I walked outside, and before I could think myself out of it, I hugged him. All I said was, "I'm sorry. I want a positive, healthy relationship." And I meant it. I did not want the marriage back; I knew we could not return to what we had been. The divorce papers were signed, the clarity was there.

But I was still searching for another way to exist inside what remained. I wanted to know what else was possible. How to rebuild something humane from the ruins.

The kids were taking pictures, smiling in a way that broke my heart. They were struggling too. They hated the division. They hated the tension.

They hated watching the two people they loved most turn into strangers who only spoke through logistics. It all felt too abrupt, too sharp. Too much for all of us.

And my tender heart could not bear the coldness of going no contact.

We softened; we became friendlier. Without realizing it, I started negotiating with myself again. *Could we be something different? Did it really have to hurt this much? Did I really have to walk all the way through the grief instead of finding a way around it?* I had just enough awareness to know the marriage was over but not enough strength yet to let myself feel everything that ending required. I was still trying to make it easier for everyone else.

A week later, I went to see an integrative medicine doctor. When I walked into her office that day, her son was sitting at a computer, deep in research. I glanced over and realized he was studying plant medicine. I asked the doctor what he was working on and whether plant medicine had played a role in her own healing.

That one question opened up a whole conversation about her encounter with what she believed were angels who watched over her. She told me how real it had been, so real that no one could ever convince her otherwise. At that point in my life I was listening for anything that pointed me back toward myself, and her words landed in a way that felt unexpectedly steady. I leaned forward in my chair, nervous and alert. I am not the plant medicine type; I am not the surrender everything type, yet something in me kept saying, *This is for you.*

The doctor helped me understand my body in ways I never had before. She explained vitamin and nutrient deficiencies I had ignored for years because slowing down had never felt safe. She pointed to a book on her shelf, and I ordered it in the car, went home, and read it straight through in one sitting. Then I watched documentaries about plant medicine and its relationship to trauma, healing, and the strange way surrender sometimes becomes clarity.

During our conversation she had mentioned casually that she was hosting a retreat. "You can come," she said. I said yes immediately. For years my greatest fear had been that stepping outside the structures I knew—marriage, ministry, and image—would cost me everything. When my marriage ended, however, it stripped me bare, and suddenly I realized there was nothing left to protect. Even as I grieved, a quieter truth emerged: I wanted to find myself apart from the woman people had applauded, the woman the church had relied on, the woman who had held everything together. I wanted *me*, and this retreat felt like another clear step forward on that path of self-discovery.

Around that same time my former husband and I found a fragile, human rhythm again, one rooted in shared history rather than in any hope for what might return. In this dynamic, we were just two people who had known each other since we were young trying to co-parent without destroying each other. And we were talking again—enough for me to mention the retreat.

He told me he did not want anything to disrupt the calm we had started to build. His voice was familiar, still persuasive in the way it had always been. But this time, I held onto me. I told him I was going.

There was no argument. No explanation. No request for permission. I simply said it, and I meant it. I could finally feel my own instincts again, and I was not willing to lose them. Not now; not again.

Part of me wondered if I should stay away from the retreat altogether, as though altering anything might destabilize a life that already felt delicate. I did not want to complicate things, though I did want to understand them.

But I went anyway, and I can say now that it became a truly meaningful part of this season of my life.

The opening ceremony of the event took place in a yoga studio after hours. I arrived on a Friday night. The space was dim and warm, and we began by setting intentions. We talked about why we were there and what we hoped to receive. As we sat together, eating lightly, I did not have to search for what I wanted. It rose up in me without effort.

I said I wanted to meet my true self, to know who I was beyond ego, beyond the ceiling I had lived beneath, and beyond the pressure that had shaped me. I wanted to understand what had happened in my life that made me lose my voice. I wanted clarity, I wanted truth, and I wanted growth.

I wanted myself.

We went home that night and returned early the next morning for breakfast, meditation, yoga, sound healing, and teaching. We were asked to wear white, marking the day as sacred. The environment felt calm and unhurried, unlike anything my nervous system had known in years. Then we were asked to step outside the room while each of us had a small pod prepared on the floor with a blanket and an eye mask.

As the other participants and I spoke together quietly while waiting, I noticed I was not afraid. I normally would have felt pronounced anxiety of doing something unfamiliar. I would feel the fear of unknown. But, the worst thing that could have happened to me already had; the bottom had already fallen out of my life. There was nothing left to fear. If this experience had something to show me, I was ready. If it wanted to teach me, I would listen.

Fear had already taken enough.

When we were invited back inside, they offered each of us a piece of plant medicine in the form of a small chocolate bar. I accepted it and lay back, trusting the process.

At first there was only heaviness. A deep settling in my body, as if I had become part of the floor itself. I felt safe. Still. Almost unable to move.

I wondered quietly what would come next. Nothing dramatic was happening, so I kept whispering that I just felt heavy and comfortable. The doctor listened, studied me, and told me she thought I was exactly where I needed to be.

Eventually, as I lay there, the first thing that came to me was a glimpse of myself in the townhouse I had moved into after leaving our family home. I saw myself in the kitchen, dancing, laughing, singing with the kids. I though, *You are really happy here. You are happy in your life. This feels good. This feels real.* The simple memory of joy washed over me.

Then everything shifted.

It felt as though color poured down from the highest point of the sky to the deepest part of the earth. Thousands of colors moving at once, full speed, all together. It was the purest form of love I had ever encountered. I could not move toward it; I could only feel it. It was overwhelming and magnificent, love without obstruction. And I understood: This is what love feels like when nothing is blocking it.

My mind moved immediately to the birth of each of my children. I cried uncontrollably as memories surfaced as embodied emotion. I saw myself holding my babies, and for the first time I felt the full reverence of that moment. A depth of love I had never fully allowed myself to feel came rushing through me, and I wept from a place I did not know existed.

Then there was a voice. Familiar, in the way sacred insight sometimes arrives from the deepest part of your own knowing. It would later strike me that under the influence of plant medicine, the ego loosens. Defenses fall away, leaving nowhere to hide from what is true.

The voice said, *You have to let go of him.*

I resisted immediately. I said *no.*

The voice returned, calm and unwavering. *This has always been your problem.*

I searched myself for some hidden wound that might explain it. Some buried trauma. Some darkness waiting to be uncovered. But when I looked inward, there was nothing concealed. Only openness. Quiet land. Green fields. No hidden pain demanding excavation.

And still the voice remained. *You have to let go of him.*

I cried. I argued. I pleaded. Why now? Even after the paperwork, after the clarity, after everything I had already lost, this was still a man I had loved deeply. A man I had fought for long after it made sense.

Letting go felt like erasing something sacred.

Then the vision shifted.

I saw my mother. Young. Light. Playful. Not the woman I had known as an adult, but who she had been before endurance reshaped her. Before *her* loyalty had demanded silence. I saw how she stayed through dark seasons, how what was called love had asked her to trade joy for stability, self for survival.

And I understood.

This was not only my story. It was an inheritance.

I saw that that my mother had stood at a similar crossroads once. She chose to stay, and that choice had shaped the rest of her life. Not all of it, but enough for me to see the cost.

I knew I was standing at my own crossroads now.

If you do not let him go, you will lose your light. You will lose your joy. You will lose yourself.

I saw the same light I had glimpsed earlier: the woman dancing in her kitchen, happy with less, but fully alive. And I knew the truth.

I cried for my mother. For what she had carried, for the loyalty to her spouse. For the parts of herself she had learned to silence to endure. And I saw how my own choices had been shaped by my observation of her: I had learned endurance before I learned freedom.

Something in me softened. Released.

I understood that what I had called a generational curse was not a curse at all: it was a pattern of protection. Silence passed down as loyalty, endurance passed down as love. I saw that I was not here to condemn it. I was here to complete it.

I said it quietly, without force: "I will let him go."

In that moment, I stepped out of inheritance and into choice. I wasn't rejecting where I came from, but I refused to carry forward what no longer belonged to me.

I saw my grandmother next. I saw the insecurities I had carried for years and understood that they were never mine. They had been absorbed through proximity, repetition, and love that did not know another way. In my truest self, I had never believed I was unworthy. That belief had been learned. Once I saw it, I could not unsee it. Now I could choose a different expression of strength.

In that room full of strangers, I let go. I could see clearly that much of my life had been shaped by pain that was never mine to hold, beliefs I had inherited without question, stories passed down out of a need to survive. I cried for hours, but in my pure essence, I was already whole.

The intensity finally softened. What remained was lightness. Ease. A sense of being at home in my body. When I opened my eyes, the doctor sat beside me and said, "You feel that?"

I did.

She told me *this* was my true self, and I did not need the medicine to return here. I could remember it, take it with me. She asked me to name the feeling.

I called it *home.*

As the room came back into focus, I realized not everyone there had the same experience. That was the point, though. My experience was not so much about the medicine as it was about timing, about having a safe place to land when my life fell apart.

I left without fireworks, but I also left without doubt. I may not have had answers about the future, but I carried something better with me. I left with myself, and that was enough to keep going. I said, "God, I trust you. Wherever you take me next, I will go." And I meant it.

After the plant medicine journey, I gathered my family around the table and shared what had come up for me in that experience. I told them about some of what I had seen, what had become painfully clear, and how much of my life had been shaped by things I had carried without fully naming. Then I turned to my father and told him what I had witnessed growing up. I told him that the way he loved my mother, the way he moved as a man in our home, had shaped my understanding of love more than I realized. What was normalized for me then became what I later tolerated. It followed me into womanhood, into marriage, into the kinds of love that asked me to adjust, endure, and disappear. I told him I could see now how much of my life had been built around patterns I first learned in that house. I was not trying to punish him. I was finally telling the truth about what it had cost me. My mother and siblings cried. I cried. My father cried too. And in that moment, I drew a line. No more. I do not want a love that feels like survival. I want a different kind of love now.

REMEMBERING THE SELF

FINDING MYSELF WHERE I LEFT HER

When everything fell away, the first thing I began to notice again was my voice. It was neither loud nor confident, just a whisper rising in the back of my throat. A truth that had been buried beneath years of duty and performance. It startled me, the sound of myself. The honesty of it. The weight of it. It felt like waking up in a body I had lived in for years but never fully occupied.

In therapy, as I named things I had never dared to say, watching my reflection and trying to recognize the woman looking back at me, I understood something quietly and clearly: rediscovery is not dramatic. It does not announce itself. It begins with the smallest act of courage in choosing to hear yourself without immediately overriding what you hear.

In the same way, I did not lose myself all at once, but gradually. For a long time survival worked, kept things moving, kept me functional, but when the house emptied—when the church was behind me, when the paperwork was filed and the noise of crisis had finally settled—I realized how unfamiliar my own breathing sounded. The systems that had once told me who I was were gone, so what remained was the responsibility of my choice.

That terrified me because I had never learned how to trust myself. Now, for the first time in my life, I could do whatever I wanted.

I realized that what I wanted more than anything was to heal.

I stopped correcting my thoughts the moment they surfaced. I stopped negotiating with my own knowing. I made a private agreement with myself to listen without punishing myself. I was no longer trying to escape anything, I was trying to understand everything.

I read constantly during the time. Books on trauma, boundaries, toxic dynamics, nervous systems, identity, voice. I watched lectures, interviews, and documentaries. I searched outward and inward at the same time, following whatever made me feel more like myself.

But as I moved, resistance followed.

This was the most traumatic season of my life, so everything felt intensified. Patterns were breaking and systems that had relied on my silence were destabilizing, leaving me to walk through something unseen without the tools I had always used. The prayers and practices that once steadied me felt hollow. I needed new ways to regulate my body, not just explain my pain.

So I learned how to meditate. How to breathe, how to sit with myself without immediately fixing anything. Some days it helped, and some days it did not. I cried often. Fear showed up in my sleep, in my home, and in the way my children responded to the uncertainty around us. Then my sister suggested I visit a small spiritual shop run by her friends.

I did not hesitate. I was too tired to be skeptical.

I walked in depleted and told them what was happening, what my home felt like, what my body felt like, how heavy everything had become. They listened without trying to correct my language or contain my experience, and then they went into the back and made a candle for me, explaining that it was meant to offer a sense of support. They also gave me another candle designed to help me release anything I was carrying that was not mine.

I went home and burned the both of the candles, and for the first time in weeks, my body softened. The fear loosened its grip.

That shift, subtle but undeniable, made me curious. I went back. I tried detox baths and more candles with specific intentions. One day I burned a self-love candle, and it turned black. They told me my self-love had to be rebuilt from the beginning. That was the first time I understood that self-love was not absent in me, but it had been interrupted.

I had spent my life inside strict spiritual boundaries, never venturing outside what was considered acceptable, but now I was seeing how many of the beliefs I had carried were rooted in fear rather than truth, in performance rather than wisdom. Without fully knowing what Reiki was, I booked a session. When the checkout page offered an add-on for a spell, I laughed and called my sister. She laughed too and said, "What do you think the candles were?" That stopped me. I realized I had already been experimenting, through a need for care and regulation rather than out of rebellion, with practices that allowed my body to feel safe enough to speak.

During the Reiki session, the practitioner paused and asked when I had stopped speaking up for myself, and the question landed deeper than anything I had prayed. This was not about rejecting God. It was about reclaiming myself. I began tracing the fracture back to its origin— in kindergarten, I talked constantly, but one day, I repeated something I did not understand the weight of, and the correction was swift. Later, as I hid in a closet, I heard words that followed me for decades:

"Myesha talks too much. Myesha needs to be quiet."

I carried that lesson forward. Around volatility and emotional instability, I learned that silence kept things calm, and eventually, my silence became instinct. Marriage then amplified what I already knew: Avoid conflict. Manage the atmosphere. Keep the peace.

Now, standing in the aftermath of divorce, I could finally see the cost. I had not just lost a life. I had lost my voice.

So I began doing the work of retrieval. Sound healing. Breathwork. Practices that moved what words never could. I cried in rooms full of strangers and did not apologize. There was a younger version of me who needed protection, and I finally understood that if she was going to be cared for, it would have to be by me.

People asked me careless questions; they could not see the cost of leaving something broken while still grieving what it once held. They assumed choosing myself should feel empowering. It did not.

But even knowing what would unravel, I would choose myself again, even though it meant rebuilding completely. The unraveling taught me something essential: every step I took, every book I read, every practice I tried, every experiment was not about becoming someone new. It was about returning.

I did not lose myself all at once. I left myself in pieces, and this was the work of gathering them back, one by one. Of coming back to my voice, my body, my truth.

Back to myself.

LEARNING HOW TO TELL THE TRUTH

The journey back to myself did not begin after everything fell apart. It had begun years earlier, quietly, long before I had language for what was breaking inside me. What would later feel like a spiritual, emotional, and psychological unraveling had already been set in motion through a multi-year formation program that asked more of me than I knew how to give. At the time, I thought I was simply trying to survive a demanding season. I did not yet understand that I was being trained to tell the truth. I could not see that honesty would become the doorway to everything that followed.

The work was rigorous and deeply human. We met in small groups of five or six, sitting in circles with people who did not know our titles, platforms, or public personas. There was no hierarchy to hide behind. We were known only through our stories, through the parts of ourselves we usually keep guarded. What emerged was awareness. When truth is hidden, it does not disappear; it settles, hardens, and divides us internally. This work confronted those hidden places and invited me into the kind of healing I needed most.

As part of the curriculum, we completed forty-eight-hour silent retreats. No phones, no music, no talking, no distractions. Just a bed, food, nature, and stillness. Forty-eight hours with nothing to perform, nothing to lead, nothing to manage. Only breath, awareness, and presence. Slowly, the dismantling of who I had learned to be, and the quiet emergence of who I truly was, began.

We mapped our lives, traced patterns, and spoke honestly about our histories and how they shaped us. Scripture and teaching guided us through the deconstruction of the selves we had built for survival and toward the reconstruction of new selves wired for wholeness. Yet for all three years of this program, I showed up without ever naming one central truth about my life. That silence remained intact, even in rooms devoted to truth.

Another requirement of the program was six months of weekly therapy. At the time I believed therapy was for people with obvious wounds; I did not yet recognize my own. Much of my pain was buried beneath competence, faith, and responsibility. I lacked language for what hurt, so it settled invisibly inside of me. I didn't think I needed therapy, but I eventually agreed to it.

I knew immediately when I found the right therapist. It wasn't about his insight; it was more that when I heard his voice, I knew he was the perfect person. It conveyed steadiness, safety, and containment, all things I needed. That first session marked the beginning of my awakening.

Week by week, I spoke about my childhood, my inner world, my fears, and the parts of myself I had never named out loud. It opened me up to tenderness I had long denied myself. Over time, a healthy, grounded trust formed between me and the therapist. He was the first adult in my life who held my story without asking me to perform, fix, or produce. He gave me one hour a week where my experience did not need justification.

That was uncomfortable for me at first. I was efficient, accomplished, and oriented toward solutions. I did not linger in feeling because feelings felt destabilizing, but therapy interrupted that reflex. It slowed me down. It taught me how to stay present with myself without fleeing what I felt.

As I grew stronger, a quiet pressure emerged within me: someone needed to know the full truth of my life. I had spent years being the container for others, but there was no one holding anything for me. Maybe it was time to trust the therapist with it. So, when the required six months ended, I kept going. Slowly, carefully, I began telling the truth in fragments. Not all at once, just enough to let air in. Moments I had minimized, words I had normalized, experiences I had quietly absorbed. And one day, after listening carefully, my therapist said, "Myesha, you put up with a lot of bullshit."

It was not judgment; it was just clarity. That sentence startled me awake because it did not soften the truth. It honored it.

Therapy helped me begin to see myself without distortion.

I began thawing, returning to myself. My voice, long restrained, started to occupy space. People thought I was already confident and bold, but these deepest parts of me had been muted for years. And as my voice strengthened, my perception of life shifted. Therapy gave me language and discernment, the ability to name reality rather than protect an image.

I continued therapy for five years. Those years, alongside graduate school, became the scaffolding that held me steady as my life changed. Prayer had carried me far, but I needed witnesses. I needed truth reflected back to me by another human.

When I traveled and spoke, I caught glimpses of the woman I was becoming: grounded, integrated, aligned. I could no longer live divided, and therapy was the bridge. Human connection was the soil of my transformation, and truth was the seed. After each session I came home with clarity and strength. I learned what real partnership, love, and self-respect required of me. The load I had carried had exceeded my capacity for years, and therapy gave me a place to lay it down. I would not have chosen therapy on my own, but I can see now that God led me there. Through education, listening, reflection, and relationship, I was guided back to myself. I had once feared being exposed, but therapy prepared me instead.

This was my awakening. Telling the truth did not begin with confrontation; it began with safety, with spaces where I was not responsible for managing anyone else's emotions, where my story could exist without a transactional exchange.

I discovered that honesty is not loud. It does not rush, it does not require an audience. It begins quietly, when you stop abandoning yourself in the name of peace. I used to believe healing required courage I did not have, but what I learned instead is that healing begins when someone is finally safe enough to stop performing. Safety comes before honesty. Voice comes after care. If you are struggling to tell the truth about your life, it may not be because you are weak; it may be because you have never been held. Before I could ask what came next, I had to ask what was true.

Maybe that is where your story begins too: not with answers, but with a place where you are finally allowed to speak. Where are you still surviving instead of naming what you know? And who, if anyone, is holding the real weight you carry?

THE GIRL I LEFT BEHIND

The girl I left behind had not disappeared all at once; she faded gradually in small negotiations I did not recognize as losses at the time. When I began asking myself where I had first learned to silence my own knowing, my mind did not go to the divorce. It did not even go to the church. It went further back, to a moment that felt small at the time but altered me in ways I couldn't comprehend.

I had sex before marriage. What followed shaped me far more than the act itself.

It was not the sex that marked me, it was the silence that came afterward—the way I learned to tuck part of myself away, how I began measuring my worth against a standard I had already failed to meet. The way I agreed, quietly and without realizing it, that some truths about me were better left unsaid.

That was the first fracture.

I became aware, almost instantly, that something about me now needed to be managed, hidden—edited. I learned how quickly a body could move from being ordinary to being suspect, and how a choice could become a shadow.

At twenty-one, I married. I stepped into the role of pastor's wife, a title that already knew who I was supposed to be, with an image to uphold. A story already written. Purity was implied, innocence was assumed. People asked directly about my virginity. Sometimes the question came softly, wrapped in admiration, but other times it came bluntly, as if entitlement had replaced discretion. There were moments I avoided answering. There were moments I did not.

I felt my chest tighten as I shaped the lie. I kept my voice even, my face calm. Each time, something subtle shifted inside me. It was not the secret that destabilized me; it was the shame. Shame did not announce itself loudly, but it settled into the corners of my body and rearranged my sense of worth. I was married, building a life, and yet I carried the quiet belief that I had forfeited something essential. There was no language for it. No space to confess without consequence, and no relief. Only the steady rehearsal of a version of myself that felt safer than the truth.

I carried that shame for years. I preached, I prayed, I fasted, I worshiped, I led; I stood on stages and spoke about faith and discipline and devotion. I helped other people find healing. None of it touched the place where I had first learned to distrust myself.

That is what unsettles me now. I learned how to be faithful without ever feeling free.

It was not until I was sitting across from a therapist—someone unafraid of my humanity—that the truth finally rose to the surface. Months into our work together, I said it out loud. Simply, without ornament. And nothing catastrophic happened.

The room did not collapse. God did not withdraw. I did not disintegrate.

Instead, something in me softened. I began to understand that what I had carried was not moral failure but inherited shame, shame absorbed from systems that confuse control with holiness and silence with virtue.

The girl I left behind was the one who believed her worth could be altered by a single act—the one who learned to split herself in order to survive, the one who agreed to disappear so that the life around her could remain intact. She had been waiting for someone to tell her she was still whole.

She had been waiting for me.

Once I began telling the truth out loud, something inside me began answering back. Throughout my healing journey, I dreamed. Not the kind of dreams that evaporate by morning; these felt deliberate, charged, symbolic. They carried the texture of memory and the weight of something unfinished. I woke up knowing they meant something even when I did not yet have language for what that something was. At the time I did not recognize them as grief. They were holding the parts of me I had lost. But I did what I had learned to do: I took them to therapy.

I would describe the images, the sensations, the emotions they left in my body when I woke up. My therapist listened carefully, helping me hear what my subconscious was trying to say, and over time, the dreams became markers. They revealed where I was in my healing journey: what was thawing, what was still buried, and what was beginning to surface. The deeper I went, the more the dreams spoke.

In one particular dream, I found myself at some sort of mixer—a room buzzing with people I knew and people I did not. It felt like a networking event, the kind you show up to in hopes of opening doors for yourself. I was trying to get my singing career off the ground, moving from person to person, smiling, nodding, trying to be seen, trying to be chosen, and I was also babysitting an infant. The baby was in a car seat, resting quietly in the car just outside the event. I do not know if I intentionally decided to leave her there or if I was moving too fast to think at all, but I left the baby in the car and rushed inside so I could make connections, shake hands, perform whatever version of myself I thought people wanted to see.

Somehow, in that dream logic that makes no sense in waking life, I drifted away from the mixer and found myself walking deeper into a completely different place. One moment I was in a crowded room full of adults in cocktail attire, and the next moment I was stepping through an archway into what looked like an amusement park. It reminded me of Knott's Berry Farm or Disneyland: loud music floating through the air, lights flashing, rides spinning, children screaming with delight. It was bright and chaotic, and I just kept moving forward, almost like my feet were running ahead of my mind.

Then suddenly it hit me—the baby. I left the baby in the car! The realization crashed into me like a wave, and I felt terror rise from the bottom of my stomach. My pulse roared in my ears, sweat pooled under my arms, panic rose until it felt like it might choke me. *You must go, now!*

I took off running, trying to retrace my steps. The park seemed bigger than before, and the paths twisted. The exits disappeared. I kept turning down corridors that dead-ended at metal gates. I cut through back alleys and staff-only areas. Even in the dream, I knew I was reliving something older than the moment. I scaled fences. I begged strangers for help, but no one helped me. They pointed vaguely in different directions, but no one took me by the hand and said, "This way." No one moved with urgency. Meanwhile, my chest tightened until it felt like a thousand elephants were sitting on me. My mind raced through everything I had learned as a registered nurse. I knew what it meant for a baby to be left inside a hot car. I knew the minutes mattered.

I finally reached the front of the park and saw the parking structure towering high above me, level after level stacked on top of each other. There was only one entrance and one exit, and I had no idea which floor I had parked on. I ran up the first ramp and then the next. I searched every level, weaving past cars and honking horns, trying to find my vehicle. A man told me to go higher. On the seventh floor, someone told me to go back down. Then, out of nowhere, a flood of water came sweeping through the structure, and I had to run to keep from being knocked off my feet. It was as though the dream wanted to drown me—like it *wanted* me to feel the full weight of being helpless, late, and lost.

I finally stumbled through a doorway that spit me out into an old school building that looked exactly like one I attended as a child: long hallways with beige tile floors. Rows of classrooms with chalkboards and metal desks. The air felt still and eerie. I moved quickly through the building and found a back exit that led me out to the parking lot—and when I got there, the scene was lit up with flashing red and blue lights.

Emergency vehicles everywhere. First responders moving quickly. My car's window shattered. I ran toward it, screaming, and saw them pulling the baby out of the car seat.

She was completely blue, limp in their hands, not breathing. They laid her on the pavement and started CPR. I fell to my knees. I prayed in the way I knew how, reaching for God from the deepest place in me. I begged,

I pleaded, *Please, God, let her live. Please. Let this baby live. I was responsible for her. I left her. I left her unattended. I failed to protect her. Please do not let her die!*

I woke up in a cold sweat, heart pounding, breath shallow.

When I told my therapist the entire dream, he sat quietly for a moment. Then he said something that split me open in a way I will never forget: "Myesha, it sounds like the baby represents you."

He put language to something I was already beginning to sense. I told him that in the dream, the baby's name was Eden. He paused and said, "Isn't it interesting that Eden represents the beginning?"

My subconscious was trying to lead me back to myself. I was running through my own life, trying to find the part of me I had left unattended, neglected, unprotected. The baby I abandoned in the dream was the girl I had abandoned in myself.

For the next two years this baby appeared repeatedly in my dreams. Not every week, not every month; sometimes six months would go by with nothing. Then suddenly I would dream again, and every time I did, I brought the dream to therapy so we could understand where I was in my healing.

Each dream marked something changing. In the next dream, I left the baby again, but this time, when I realized she was missing, I ran back sooner. I felt panic, but I also felt determination. I was quicker, more aware, more connected. Then another dream: the baby had been born in a hospital, and when I went to retrieve her, she was gone. Someone had taken her. I stormed through the hallways, demanding answers, furious, protective, unwilling to accept her disappearance. My therapist said, "Myesha, you are caring now. You were not caring for yourself before. You left her once without thought. Now you are fighting for her."

As the dreams evolved, so did I. In one dream I found toddlers wandering alone in a hallway of a hotel, children left unattended. I did not abandon them or run away; I stood by the wall and kept watch until help came. It was symbolic of the way I was becoming present to myself—protective, aware.

Another dream: I held the baby in my arms. I cried over her. I could feel her heartbeat against my chest. I could feel the love pouring out of me. I was connected, attuned, awake.

These dreams became spiritual markers for me, signposts of who I had been and who I was becoming. Every dream became a reflection of where I stood in my own healing, how well I was caring for myself, and how deeply I had learned to honor the girl I once abandoned. The baby was always me. What I had never named before as loss was the quiet abandonment of my own becoming: The girl who learned to stay quiet. The girl who learned to wait. The girl who learned that her needs were negotiable and her presence optional. No one had ever told me that losing yourself counts as grief. There was no funeral, no ritual, no language for it at all. So my body dreamed what my mouth could not yet say.

Eden was always me.

One weekend when the kids were gone, the house was silent in a way I had never known. I sat alone on the floor of my daughter's room and began to cry. Hollowly. The kind of crying that comes when adrenaline finally leaves the body. As I cried, one thought repeated itself: *The love you are looking for—give it to yourself. Love yourself.*

I realized I had no idea what that meant. I had spent my life loving others through service, endurance, and responsibility. Loving myself felt abstract, undefined, almost suspicious.

But stuck with it. I wrapped my arms around myself, awkwardly at first. I said out loud that I was enough, that I was worthy. The words felt foreign. I cried harder. "I will never leave," I said. "I will take care of you. I love you, Myesha."

That afternoon turned into journaling—pages of questions for myself that I had never asked. *What makes you lovable? How can I show you love? Who has ever truly loved you?*

That weekend did not bring healing, or joy, but it did bring honesty. I did not fall in love with myself. I met myself.

HEALING WHAT I ABANDONED

I had been doing the soul work quietly, peeling back layers, learning to hear my own voice again. Then one afternoon, on an Instagram Live, a wellness coach I followed mentioned she was taking a small group of women to Bali. I responded before my mind could intervene: *I am going!*

The timing was precise—it was my first wedding anniversary after the divorce was final. My first summer alone. The same week my old life used to mark and celebrate. Standing at the intersection of who I had been and who I was becoming, I chose the road that frightened me most.

Bali held me before I even touched the ground. The thick air and warm rain met me like old friends, as though this place knew me before I knew myself. I did not cross the world looking for escape or distraction; I came looking for the woman I had misplaced, and the moment my feet touched the tiles outside the airport, I knew I was standing somewhere that remembered me even when I did not remember myself.

That first night I slept deeply, partly from jet lag, but mostly from relief. Just before sunrise I woke to roosters crowing, rain tapping softly against the roof, and the quiet hum of life moving around me. I opened the curtains and watched the sun rise over the rice paddies as I lay still, listening to my breath and heartbeat. It felt like a new beginning, steady and sure. As light filled the room, I softened. I realized I could be here alone and still be whole. Tears came, tears of pure gratitude. I was walking through one of the hardest seasons of my life, and I was still standing, still alive, still open.

For the first time in a long time, I exhaled fully.

Even now I can feel it in my body: the texture of the sheets against my skin, the steady hum of the air conditioner. The spaciousness of the room holding me. There was emptiness, yes, but there was also a fullness I had never learned how to claim before. This time I was giving myself what I had spent years seeking elsewhere—presence. Care. Compassion. Support.

That morning taught me something simple and profound: I could be complete without anything else proving it.

In the days that followed, the land continued to meet me gently. I had planned to see a Balinese healer on the day of my wedding anniversary. I needed to mark the date differently this year. For years my body was accustomed to leaving the country on that date; travel had become muscle memory. This time, I wanted the day to belong to me.

When I arrived for the session, the healer asked me not to overexplain. Instead, he looked at me with quiet attentiveness and spoke in a way that felt less like instruction and more like acknowledgement. I realized how long it had been since I felt spiritually seen without being asked to give something in return. I was used to voices that spoke about God while benefiting from my labor, and this was different. This man spoke to the places in me that had gone unnoticed for years.

He named my open heart, the depth of my love. He told me, in his understanding of the world, that I carried power I had not yet learned how to use. He spoke about the life ahead of me as an invitation to trust myself enough to step forward. What mattered was not the accuracy of his words so much as how they landed. They reached places that had been starving for care.

This was the first time I chose an experience without filtering it through fear or religious permission. For most of my life conformity had been the price of belonging, but sitting there with the healer, I felt the quiet relief of choosing myself without apology or justification.

The emotion came all at once. I cried deeply from a place beneath language. It felt as though life itself was meeting me where I had been most alone. When the healer said, "You have good energy. You just do not yet know how to use it," I sensed possibility. He blessed me in his own way, according to his culture and tradition. He prayed in a language I did not understand, but meaning did not require translation. I received it.

Afterward, something settled in me. It was grounding. For the first time in decades, I felt held, not by a person, a church, or a role, but by life itself.

Bali became an altar in the middle of my unraveling, a place where I was not a wife or a First Lady or a pastor or a mother managing crisis. I was simply myself. And that was enough. Bali gave me permission— permission to trust my body, permission to listen to my knowing, and permission to stop asking external systems to validate what my spirit had already confirmed. I did not come back with a plan. I came back with myself.

On the last day, as I packed my suitcase and sat on the edge of the bed letting the trip settle into my body, my brother sent me a link. Just a simple YouTube video, a man talking about how he built his channel. I watched it quietly, and when it ended, I knew. *When you go home, you are going to start a YouTube channel. You are going to tell your story. It is time.*

I had spent a year in silence, a year swallowing my truth. A year protecting everyone but myself. And now, after the sunrise and the land and the blessing and the permission I had received, I was ready to speak.

When I boarded the plane to leave Bali, I was not the same woman who had arrived. I was softer. Clearer. My peace was no longer borrowed from structure. It was my own. I did not know what my life would look like next, but I knew this: I was not going to disappear again. Something had been reborn in Bali, and when the wheels touched the runway at the airport back home, I was ready to begin.

Awakening demands action. The land had opened me, and the truth had found me. Now I had to live as the woman I had met. When I came home, the old life waited for me, asking one question: *What are you going to do now?*

And for the first time, my answer rose without fear: *Use my voice.*

WHAT IT COST TO SPEAK

There is a moment in every woman's healing when something quiet but unmistakable rises inside her. It is rarely convenient. It begins as a whisper she tries to ignore, then returns with more insistence. A voice she has never fully trusted before. Her own.

What follows is the slow, destabilizing realization that the life you built to survive can no longer hold the truth you are beginning to hear. Choosing yourself does not arrive as a celebration; it arrives as a reckoning.

After the awakening, after the grief, after the clarity Bali placed in my hands, I believed I was ready. I thought choosing myself would feel like freedom, but instead, it felt like rupture. The ground shifted beneath me, and nothing I had relied on remained intact. That season stripped away my ability to keep performing. I stopped bending myself into shapes that made others comfortable, I stopped swallowing truths that were quietly hollowing me out. I saw, with painful clarity, that the strategies that once kept me safe had become the walls that confined me.

The work was about no longer disappearing. It required me to confront the places where I had been diminished, erased, and taught to tolerate what made me feel unsafe. It demanded boundaries sharp enough to sever the illusions I had used to keep functioning. It asked me to choose honesty even when honesty dismantled everything I thought made me valuable.

Sometimes protection looks like collapse; sometimes everything must fall apart so you can finally stand. Loving my children meant showing them a mother who was alive, not preserved by silence. I began to understand that safety is holy, joy is holy, and choosing yourself is not selfish. It is a form of truth telling.

I made a series of choices without applause: speaking honestly when silence would have been easier: letting go of people, roles, and stories I once needed to survive. I walked away from the only world I had ever known because staying would have required abandoning myself again.

This was the moment when the woman I had always been stopped waiting for permission and came back for myself. I stopped protecting everyone else and learned how to protect myself. I reclaimed my voice, my power, my body, my finances, my desire, and my center. I rose from the debris of a life that demanded my silence and chose to live differently. Alive. Awake.

Whole.

When I arrived at home, I texted my videographer and told him I was ready to work. I simply said, "I want to do a YouTube channel," and he immediately said yes. We scheduled filming for the following week. I had no script, no outline, no clear plan for how the pieces of my story would come together. I only knew I needed to show up as the woman I was becoming. I trusted that everything I had untangled in therapy and in my everyday life would rise and speak for me.

Recording day arrived, and the videographer moved through my home, setting up lights and cameras as I transformed my living room into a small studio. I chose a simple pink dress that felt soft against my skin and allowed me to breathe. My hair was in a short bob I had cut as part of reclaiming myself. I did my own makeup with the same hands that had wiped tears, cooked meals, written devotionals, and held my children through grief. The ease of it all felt like confirmation. I was exactly where I was meant to be. This moment had been preparing me long before I knew it was coming.

He clipped the microphone to my dress, and I sat down. The camera light turned red, and I began.

I spoke for nearly thirty minutes without stopping. There were no cuts, no retakes, no corrections. It was one continuous flow of truth. I told the story from beginning to end, and I shared the parts I had once been afraid to hear myself say aloud. I owned what belonged to me. I acknowledged what I had tolerated. I spoke about the woman I had been in the marriage and the woman I was choosing to become. For the first time in a long while, I felt fully aligned with myself. This was no performance, no shaping of my voice to fit a role.

Yet I was intentional about not disparaging my former husband. I understood what his reputation meant to him and how central it had been to many arguments, conflicts, and moments where I felt pressure to remain silent. Touching that would have been easy, but I chose restraint. My healing required honesty, not destruction. I could tell my story without dismantling his character; I could speak my truth without stepping outside my integrity.

When we finished, we edited the footage and chose a release date. All of it felt meaningful and aligned with the rebirth I was experiencing. I created a simple graphic announcing that I would be sharing my divorce story on my YouTube channel and scheduled it to go live on Sunday at six in the evening, two days before the video itself.

That same Sunday evening, I attended a wedding for a longtime church member. It was one of the first public events where my former husband and I were both present, and people did not know how to engage with me. Their expressions were tight and cautious; they were still living in the world I had left, a world where my absence required explanation. I stood alone at the reception, scrolling on my phone but standing tall. My confidence came from a place I had never accessed before. If anyone had known the full weight of what I had carried privately, they would have understood every choice I was making, and that awareness steadied me.

At six o'clock, my announcement went live on social media. I felt the energy in the room shift. People glanced at their phones and then looked at me. They whispered. They stared. Some approached with questions disguised as concern: they wanted to know what I was going to say, how much I would share, whether I would reveal something they were not prepared to hear.

My former husband sat across the room. When I walked nearby before leaving, he spoke to me quickly, his tone tight and urgent. He said he felt blindsided; he repeated familiar refrains about how he understood the marriage and his role in it. He expressed confusion about why I would share my story publicly, said it felt harmful to him.

His words were measured, but the intensity beneath them was unmistakable, and my body recognized the moment for what it was. I listened. I stood still. And something terrible in me woke up.

Bali had opened me. The healer had blessed me; the land had held me like a mother. But as I stood there face-to-face with the man who had shaped the narrative for so long, something rose within me.

My heart pounded as familiar instincts surfaced: *Keep the peace. Do not escalate. Make yourself smaller. Protect the story so nothing worsens.* My body remembered those years of survival, and for a moment I felt the pull to retreat—to cancel the video, to quiet myself again. To pretend none of this was happening.

Then another voice rose within me, one clearer and steadier than fear. It was the truest version of myself—the one that had waited beneath years of accommodation. She spoke plainly: *This ends now. I am done disappearing. I am done shrinking. If I silence myself here, I will spend the rest of my life negotiating my own existence, and I will never step into the life God has been calling me toward. I will share this from my lived experience to tell the truth as I experienced it.*

This was the moment I stayed with myself as an *action*. Here I understood that my voice was not optional. It was essential. It had carried me through survival, and it would now carry me into the life I had been praying for, a life I could not reach without crossing this threshold.

I walked away from my former husband disoriented, caught between old reflexes and new resolve, yet knowing with certainty that there was no version of me that could return to silence. My hands shook. Doubt crept in as my nervous system searched for familiar order. I replayed the conversation, reminding myself that I was not attacking anyone, that I was simply telling my own story. More fear surfaced about possible consequences—disruption, instability. All those quiet punishments women learn to anticipate when they stop cooperating.

And still, beneath the fear, something steadier held. Something truer. Something that would not let me turn back. *Do it anyway.*

What was awakening inside me was older than this moment—older than a video, older than a marriage ending. It lived in my nervous system and in the inherited instincts of women who survived by shrinking, by staying quiet, by carrying stories that never reached the light. This was not only about uploading a video, it was about breaking a lineage of silence. It was about becoming the woman I had never seen but always needed: a woman who could speak openly, live truthfully, and remain rooted in herself without asking permission. I had never seen that modeled, so I chose to model it. For my children, and for those who would come after them. They would know how to stand, how to speak, and how to live whole instead of hidden.

I was speaking for the generations behind me and the generations ahead of me, for the younger version of myself who learned that quiet felt safer than truth. For the versions of me who survived by shrinking and made it through, but never lived fully free. I could feel them with me, steadying me, asking me not to turn away again. Whatever followed, whatever reactions came, I knew I was no longer willing to retreat. I believed deeply that I had a right to speak. A right to hold an opinion. A right to exist as an individual. A right to live inside my own body without permission. This was about agency, about gathering the parts of myself that had learned to stay small, to stay safe, and saying, *Stand up.*

I understood that choosing truth would cost me something, but silence had already cost me far more. I was done negotiating my existence, done shrinking to preserve someone else's comfort. Whatever this choice demanded, I was willing to meet it. I was no longer available for disappearance.

In the days leading up to the video's release, my body stayed on high alert. Anxiety surged. My thoughts raced. I paced through the house like a woman trying to discharge electricity from her veins. Everything in me wanted to retreat, to make myself smaller again, to return to whatever felt safest—that was the version of me that knew how to endure.

But another version of me was also present now: the woman I was becoming. The woman God had been shaping patiently over time. She stood steady and grounded. I felt myself being retrained in real time, learning a new way to respond. *This is how you rise*, she whispered. *By moving forward even when your knees are shaking.*

My body panicked because it had never been asked to take up this much space before. It had never been invited to honor itself while disrupting a familiar pattern. Even so, I sensed a future version of myself nearby, calm and steady, offering quiet instruction. *Let me show you how to stay here now.* And I felt God with me as presence.

Truth stood at my back, fear in front of me. This time, I chose truth.

I knew that telling this story was not something I had manufactured; it rose from prayer, discernment, and a deep internal knowing. When it did, I said yes. I trusted what was awakening inside me. I knew there would be no undoing it. It would mark the end of one chapter and the beginning of another: an end to silence, an end to pretending, an end to carrying someone else's image at the expense of my own voice.

With every younger version of myself present, and with the weight of generations of quiet endurance behind me, I pressed *upload*. There was no spectacle. Only resolve.

When I returned home that night, my phone began to light up. Messages arrived from every direction. Some were supportive; some were harsh. Some attempted to pressure me back into quiet.

I did not engage. I set boundaries, blocked what needed to be blocked, and kept moving forward. By then I already knew there was no path back.

The following day, the video went live on my own platform. My heart pounded, but I felt steady. Then something unexpected happened: it spread. People watched, shared, responded. The story moved beyond me. I had no plan for that, no expectations it would do so. I had simply told the truth as it lived in my body and released it.

The public response reflected something I had not fully accepted yet: I was powerful. I had simply spent much of my life withholding that power from myself. As the hours passed and the numbers climbed, something else followed: Relief. Peace. A quiet freedom I had never known. The fear that had followed me for years began to loosen its grip.

What surprised me most was how simple the act felt once it was done. It was just the truth, spoken and allowed to breathe. I had spent much of my life afraid of doing exactly what I had just done. Standing on the other side of it, I realized there was nothing left to protect except myself. And for the first time, I knew how. I had not only shared an experience; I had reclaimed my voice, and once a woman claims her voice, she cannot return to the version of herself who needed permission to exist.

I wrestled with wanting to protect my children from details and disruption. The divorce had been final for some time, and I wanted stability for them—less upheaval, more grounding. At the same time, I wanted them to witness what it looks like when a woman stands even while afraid, when she tells the truth, when she chooses herself. I wanted them to know that something had ended and that something more honest and life-giving was being born.

Releasing the video also meant risking my standing within the faith community and upsetting people who had watched us from a distance—people who trusted me, people who believed the story they had already been told. I knew I risked being misunderstood, mischaracterized, and quietly judged. Once I spoke out, I could no longer control how my story would be received. Still, I chose to honor my voice.

When you face the thing you fear most and wake up unchanged, it alters you. Courage, I learned, is not a thought: it is a presence you inhabit.

And even as the moment carried triumph, it carried grief. I continued to grieve the life that would never return, even the version of myself who kept secrets in the name of peace. At the same time, I honored the woman who finally allowed that version to rest.

Both were true.

DISCERNMENT AND DESIRE

THE RETURN

When the video was finally out in the world and the noise around me began to settle, something unexpected happened. Instead of collapsing into fear, I found myself landing in a place where I had not stood for a very long time. It felt like muscle memory, like returning to a room my body remembered even if my mind had forgotten how to name it.

Since childhood I had sensed God in a visceral way. Before language, before responsibility, before anyone explained who God was supposed to be, I felt Him. A quiet knowing lived within me, a deep spiritual sensitivity that felt innate, like breath or intuition or hunger. It was not something I learned; it was something I arrived on this earth with. Over time that sensitivity didn't disappear, but it got crowded out. I learned to second-guess it, to check it against other voices. I learned to ask permission before trusting what rose naturally inside me. I didn't stop knowing, but I stopped listening.

After I posted the video, the space between me and God felt thin again, as if I could finally hear Him once more beneath the static. It wasn't that God had returned, it was that I stopped bracing myself long enough to feel Him.

What surprised me most was the clarity: My intuition felt awake. My discernment felt embodied. For the first time in years I was not translating my knowing through fear or obligation. I realized then that what I had been losing was not faith, it was the belief that someone else needed to authorize what I already knew.

One afternoon I sat on the bench by the sliding glass door of my house and noticed something that brought me up short: I had not listened to worship music in many months. It had been too painful. Worship was where I had always met God most intimately before, and after everything I had walked through, I couldn't bear to go there again. I shut that part of myself down to survive. Today, though, I had just returned home from Atlanta. I had gone to church there and felt something stir, but it wasn't until I was alone, back in my own quiet, that the moment came.

I pulled up songs I used to sing—songs my body knew way back when. I pressed play, and when I heard the first note, I wept, wept from somewhere deep. My breath hitched, my chest convulsed. Sound came out of me before I decided to make it. I sang through tears, loud, uncontained. Alone. My voice cracked, and I kept going anyway. It felt like my soul was being resuscitated, like oxygen was rushing back into places that had been deprived of breath for years. I sang and cried for hours.

This return had nothing to do with roles, platforms, or ministries. It was a pure return to God—the God I had known as a child, the God who met me when I had no words. The God who held my children. The God who stayed when everything familiar fell away. The God who carried me when I had nothing left to carry myself with.

In that moment, my connection to God was restored, without obligation or performance, but as relationship. I realized I needed God for myself.

A steadiness moved through me that day. My posture changed. I stopped reaching for God out of fear or duty and started reaching out of trust. I stopped asking who I needed to be to deserve His presence and rested in the truth that I had never been outside of it. I no longer felt the need to explain myself or seek permission to trust what I sensed inside.

I understood something simple and grounding then: the next chapter of my life was no longer about surviving what had happened to me. It was about learning to trust the leading in my own heart. I was not rebuilding a life; I was returning to myself.

THE AWAKENING OF DESIRE

When I stepped away from the ministry side of my life, I did not leave the building all at once. For a season I continued working inside those same walls as the manager of the church's venue I co-founded. I stayed because I was disentangling; my life was rearranging faster than my nervous system could keep up with, and I needed a place where my body still knew how to move. Work was one of the few environments where I felt oriented, but I was going through the motions without any sense of belonging.

Overseeing the venue felt empowering. I was no longer standing on stages or managing spiritual atmospheres; instead, I was in meetings, on corporate calls, working alongside executives and production teams who had no expectations for who I was supposed to be beyond competent and clear. It was grounding, in a way.

One of the larger events the church hosted during that time carried significant responsibility and visibility, and the buildup was intense. I was communicating with the event producer primarily through email, however, and everything felt standard and contained. Our interactions had no sense of anticipation or emotional investment attached. It was just work.

A few days before the event, we held a walkthrough with the security detail and key team members. I opened the front door of the venue, and the event producer walked in. He introduced himself easily, confident in himself, present to the moment. We had been communicating through email for months. We exchanged names, he smiled—and my body responded before my mind could catch up.

It startled me.

This was the first time since my marriage that I felt attraction toward another man, and the sensation surprised me with its intensity. It wasn't subtle; it moved through me like a current, sudden and undeniable. I felt awake in places that had been quiet for a long time. My shoulders drew back without conscious effort, my breath deepened, and my stomach fluttered in that unmistakable way that signals recognition before thought catches up. I remember thinking, almost in wonder, *I'm alive. I'm really alive.* I was single, he was attractive, and something in his presence felt steady and self-contained—the kind of groundedness that invites rather than demands.

I felt myself leaning into the moment. There was a warmth to it, a softness, a sense of ease that surprised me. I wasn't trying to impress or manage the exchange, and I wasn't measuring myself or performing. I simply noticed how my body responded—how relaxed I felt standing near this man, how natural it was to be seen without bracing. Then, at some point, a quiet question surfaced, almost like a whisper: *Wait . . . is he married?*

My eyes scanned his hand.

There was a ring.

The realization landed with a dull ache, a brief deflation I felt in my chest. *Of course*, I thought. *Of course he is.* The moment didn't shatter, but it did close. Gently and cleanly, the way a door does when you understand it was never meant to open.

What surprised me was how intact I remained. I didn't fold in on myself, I didn't feel embarrassed or undone. The attraction didn't turn chaotic or painful; it simply became information. He didn't stay with me, but what my body had revealed did: that desire could rise without overtaking me, that connection didn't have to come with urgency or loss of control, and that my nervous system could register interest and still feel safe.

The following day during the event setup, that same grounded energy was there. He was attentive, present, and when I stepped away to take my children to choir practice and returned hours later, he remembered and asked how it had gone. My body exhaled. No one had asked me something like that in a long time.

During the event I stood upstairs alone, watching the room. At one point he came and stood nearby. There was no conversation. No agenda. Just proximity. That was enough to tell me everything. It was my first real experience of standing inside my own adult morality, heeding my own compass. I was no longer making decisions based on rules handed to me by marriage, religion, or fear. I was deciding as a woman who owned her life, and I found I could feel attraction and remain anchored. Desire did not hijack me; it informed me. Desire was instructional.

It showed me that desire did not require action to be real—and that integrity was not the absence of longing, but the presence of choice. Feeling attraction did not feel like betrayal; rather, it was evidence that my body was awake, responsive, and trustworthy again. I remember taking a mental snapshot of that moment and saying to myself, *In the right time and in the right way, I want to feel this again.* It did not change my circumstances or alter my decisions, but it shifted my understanding: I was still here, awake beneath the surface, and capable of discernment.

That awareness followed me through the church building I still entered, through the work I still performed, and through the parts of my life I called temporary while quietly negotiating permanence. Once something wakes up in you, it becomes impossible not to notice where you are still making compromises with the past, whether for closeness or safety, connection or choice. Around that same time I listened to other women's stories: divorced women and former pastors' wives. There were stories of weekends away, of passion, of being wanted again, of hot girl summers and freedom that felt electric. I listened with curiosity, even humor; I wanted my own version of that release. I kept waiting for the invitation, for the moment where desire would rush forward and demand expression. Over time, I wondered if something in me was late . . . or simply precise.

It never arrived the way I expected.

When desire did return, urgency did not. For the first time in my life I noticed the difference. What I wanted most was internal alignment, self-trust, and I had spent too many years overriding my inner knowing in the name of closeness. I had confused intimacy with access. I had given my body away before to preserve peace, and I was not willing to do that again.

So I made a decision that surprised even me: I chose abstinence.

This movement was rooted in devotion to myself, shaped by care for my healing, respect for my timing, and trust in the woman I was becoming. I wanted to move forward without fracturing myself again; I wanted to know that when intimacy came, it would arrive at a body that trusted itself.

This was not easy for me. I want to be clear about that. This was not the choice of a woman disconnected from desire—it was the choice of a woman who felt it fully and still chose herself. I learned how to sit with impulse without acting on it, how to let attraction exist without turning it into a whole story. How to feel longing without letting it lead. During that season, one sentence stayed with me and became an anchor: *I am not willing to give up what I want most for what I want now.*

Every day, I chose myself in quiet ways. I learned what safety felt like inside my own body, and I learned how to be alone without being lonely. I learned how to let desire refine rather than drive me. *This* was agency.

Years have passed, and I am still standing inside that decision. I have not crossed even the smallest physical line—not even a kiss—and I say that without shame or apology. Abstinence became a practice of self-trust rather than a measure of virtue, and that choice has protected my healing. It's kept me honest, and it has taught me the difference between desire that asks to be consumed and desire that asks to be honored.

THE FINAL THREAD

When my role within the church ended, I was at peace with that conclusion, but The Commons was different. It felt more functional, my vision in practice. When we purchased the building, one side of the operation became the ministry, and the other was developed into a venue. The sanctuary belonged to the church, but the venue was a separate operational arm, one I was asked to lead. I helped shape its structure and assemble its systems, translating a blank space into a working business. I collaborated where approval was required, but the day-to-day design, operations, staffing, workflows, and revenue strategy were stewarded by me. It became my entrepreneurial expression housed inside a ministry campus.

After stepping away from church life, I returned to The Commons to run the venue while I navigated divorce. I needed stability and income; I had no retirement and no stable financial safety net, and this ecosystem had been part of my economic identity for some time. I knew it, and it knew me. So I continued running the venue independently.

Then one day, my role was terminated. This time it came in writing. It also came through someone other than my former husband. I accepted it without argument. My body had recognized the ending before my thoughts could catch up. But the replacement they hired did not last. I was asked to consult, maintain operations, and support the transition. I said yes.

For several more months I showed up. We hosted large-scale events: weddings, concerts, and conferences. Everything ran smoothly because

I was still there; I knew every inch of that space, the systems, the vulnerabilities, the fail-safes, and the strengths of the team.

But the cost for me was steep. When they brought me back as a consultant, the role had shifted in ways that no longer aligned with the level of responsibility I was carrying. At first I accepted it because I needed time—time to heal, time to think, time to rebuild. But the longer I stayed, the clearer something became: The math no longer made sense. Not financially, not ethically, and not internally.

I had built this. I had given my brilliance, my labor, my creativity, and my sacrifice. Now I saw how easily I had continued to give without reassessing what it was costing me. The questions came quietly but persistently: *Why am I still here? Why am I holding together something that no longer holds me? Why am I delaying a future I keep saying I want?*

The truth was simple and difficult. The Commons was the last thing tethering me to my former life, and leaving meant severing the final thread. But my willingness was gone. No more shared responsibilities. No more reasons to stay connected. No more easy explanations for proximity.

Leaving also carried real risk because my resume confused people: I was an executive without corporate experience and a nurse who had not practiced in years, an entrepreneur without a conventional path. I thought about rent, gas, groceries, and I thought about failure. I thought about starting over at an age when I had assumed life would be settled.

Still, something deeper was true: staying was costing me my future. I could not expand here. I could not be public, creative, or fully myself in that environment. I could not build what was coming while remaining anchored to what had trained me to shrink. I loved the work, and I loved the team; The Commons was my baby. But loving something does not mean you stay when it requires you to disappear.

I drafted a letter ending my work relationship. I trained the people who would take over. I had the honest conversations. And I did not linger. I understood that leaving would be the hardest decision of my adult life, yet it was the decision that would change everything. It told my soul she mattered, it told my future it was allowed to arrive, and it told my children that self-respect is not optional.

I did not yet know what would come next. I only knew I could no longer build my future inside a place that required my silence. Leaving The Commons was not an ending; it was authorship, and once I chose that, there was no going back.

THE END OF WHAT WAS

In time, I found her: the version of me I had left behind. The girl who gave the credit away to everyone else when she was the muscle behind it all. It was time for the real me to stand up.

These fragments in me needed to be reclaimed. I had to say to myself, *Myesha, you were this before you ever met this man. He did not create this; you carried it before him. You found a way. You made it happen.* Was I blessed to have built beautiful things in partnership? Yes. But this essence was me all along.

Remembering who I had always been changed everything. When I laid out every job, every hustle, every reinvention, every business I had built with my bare hands, I had to face the truth I had avoided for most of my adult life: I had never been the supporting cast. I was the engine. I was the one who had made impossible things look effortless. Yet somewhere along the way, I let a man, a ministry, and a marriage slowly teach me to doubt this. I traded my genius for approval, my voice for peace. I traded the fullness of who I was for the hope of being loved.

Reclaiming myself was not just about remembering what I could do; it also confronted the ways I had abandoned myself to belong to a life that could not hold me. This return to what I had buried is where my reclamation truly began because once I saw who I had always been, I could never go back to pretending I was smaller than that.

From here on, everything I rebuilt—my voice, my boundaries, my work, and my future—would rise from this clarity. I am the source. I always was. This is the truth that made every next step possible, the truth that finally brought me home to myself. I did not know then that what I was saying goodbye to was not just a place, but the version of myself who had learned to survive there.

I saved the stage for last.

I walked through the building in silence, floor by floor, light by light, room by room, touching the walls I had once painted with vision. I paused in the spaces where I had spent years solving impossible problems, holding up whole worlds, and making miracles look casual. I walked past the lobby where brides had cried on my shoulder. I walked the hallways where staff members had asked questions only I could answer. I walked through the green room where performers had paced back and forth, trusting that I had every detail under control.

But the stage was the one place I could not avoid, the one spot I could not pass without acknowledging what it had been to *me.*

It was forty feet wide—the only part of the venue that did not shift or change or get rolled into the corner. I had ordered it, approved the installation. I knew its weight, its height, its feel under my feet. I knew how it held people, and I remembered how it had held me. It held up my competence, my leadership, my vision. It had been the last place where I could look out and say, "This is what I built. This is what I held together. This is what I made possible."

I walked up the steps slowly. I sat on the edge. I let my feet dangle over the side, and I let the quiet surround me. This was the last time I would ever sit here as the woman who had carried so much of herself here. Tears came before I could stop them.

I looked around at the empty room and whispered, "Thank you for everything. Thank you for every late night. Thank you for every solution that only I could find. Thank you for carrying me through my grief when I had nowhere else to go. Thank you for being the one visible thing in my life that made me feel like my work mattered."

I thanked the stage for the future I had once imagined here, and for the stability I thought it would give me. For the legacy I thought I was building. I thanked it for the clients, the staff, the weddings, the concerts, and the nights when the entire building had vibrated with energy while I was the one who made it all look effortless.

And then I had to thank it for the truth. The truth that staying would stop me.

This stage could not hold the woman I was becoming.

I sat on the edge of it, breathing through the ache in my chest, and I let the final goodbye rise up in me.

I was not just leaving a job. I was severing the last tie to a life that had kept me small. I was walking away from a place that looked successful on the outside but cost me my soul on the inside. I was closing the only door left that kept me connected to my past.

I touched the stage one last time, ran my fingers over the finishing I had chosen, and felt my own power return to my body—the same power I had when I was that girl who hustled and figured things out. The same girl who skated across bridges, solved problems nobody else could solve, and built her life from sweat and instinct.

She had returned. She was here. And she was leading now.

I stood up. I looked out over the empty venue. I whispered, "I release you. And I release the version of me who needed you."

Then I walked off the stage where I had once placed my worth. For the first time in twenty years, I walked into a future that belonged only to me.

AUTHORSHIP

THE WOMAN WHO MOVED MOUNTAINS AND SEAS

Stepping away from The Commons forced me to look honestly at who I had been inside that world. This was the chapter where that woman finally came into view.

I had been the one people called when something went wrong, when something broke, when something needed to be fixed immediately. I was the one who steadied every crisis, anticipated problems before they surfaced, and held the entire operation together without asking for acclaim or relief. The public saw a polished venue; they never saw the nights I saved events that should have collapsed.

That is the version of me people still do not understand: the woman who solved high-stakes problems quietly, who carried complexity without visibility, whose competence was assumed—and whose presence was treated as optional. Yet before I ever learned to say no, long before I reclaimed the woman I had abandoned, I had already been someone who could move mountains in silence. The world never asked her what it cost.

There was one night that crystallized it: We were hosting a major, high-visibility event at The Commons. A globally known artist was performing during an international gathering, and people were flying in from around the world. Industry leaders, executives, and partners were all present. Every detail mattered, and failure was not an option. I oversaw the entire operation: contracts, vendors, production schedules, staffing, risk. Everything was aligned. When the decision-makers arrived for the final walkthrough, the venue was ready.

Then I stepped away briefly to handle an unrelated issue elsewhere in the building.

While I was gone, a woman from the city entered the venue. She raised her voice at the staff. She told the client the event could not happen due to a permitting issue. She moved through the building, asserting authority, creating panic. By the time I returned, the staff looked shaken. Someone handed me the woman's phone number and told me what had happened.

It was 5:30 p.m., and the doors were scheduled to open at 8:00. Hundreds of people were already en route. The client had invested heavily. The entire night depended on what happened next. Inside me something tightened, but on the outside, I was calm, quiet, and steady. Years of experience in nursing came back online. My body knew how to respond under pressure.

I made the call. I introduced myself and asked how I could help. The woman on the other end of the line explained that the event could not proceed. I listened, and then I calmly walked her through the permitting process we had followed. I named the department involved and explained the approval timeline.

There was a pause. The department I worked with closed at four on Fridays. Now she could not verify anything, and she could not escalate. By the time she had arrived earlier, it had already been too late.

She hung up.

The event went on. Guests arrived, the artist took the stage, and the night unfolded without disruption. No one knew how close everything had come to collapsing—except for me.

That night did not make me powerful. It reminded me of what I had survived. I had learned to function at that level by disappearing inside competence. I stayed calm because I had trained myself to absorb pressure without reaction. I knew what to say because I had learned how to read systems quickly and move quietly through them. The steadiness people relied on was not strength alone; it was vigilance and containment. It was a nervous system trained to stay upright no matter the cost.

What I mistook for capability was also self-erasure. For years, having power had meant holding everything without being seen, solving problems without needing anything back, and carrying weight without leaving a trace. I was trusted because I did not require attention. I was valued because I did not disrupt the system that depended on me staying small.

That was not resilience, that was survival, and survival had a cost.

Over time I began to see that the same strength that made me indispensable had also made me invisible. I was treated as optional because I had trained people to rely on my disappearance. That realization changed how I understood power. Now power no longer requires me to disappear to be effective. I do not need to prove my worth by absorbing more, and I do not need to justify my place through endurance. I no longer need to hold the entire system together to earn belonging.

Leaving The Commons was not a rejection of my strength; it was a refusal to keep using it in ways that cost me my body, my voice, and my future. I left because responsibility without agency is another form of erasure.

Still, the cost was real. The Commons was my entrepreneurial expression. I had helped build it from the ground up. I carried the institutional memory. When I was present, operations stabilized, and when I stepped away, things unraveled.

Yet, when I was brought back as a consultant, the rate I received no longer reflected the scope of my responsibility. I could feel where I was still shrinking. I could feel where my future was being quietly traded for familiarity. I could feel the cost in my body long before I admitted it in my mind. What I had lived through was not only emotional or spiritual; it was physical, and my body had learned to survive by staying alert, guarded, and restrained. What I called strength my nervous system experienced as threat.

For a long time I couldn't read what my body was trying to tell me. Eventually I did some specialized testing. A doctor reviewed the results and explained what I had not wanted to see: my hormones were dangerously low—all of them. My body looked decades older than it should have. Years of living in constant fight-or-flight had taught my system to survive by powering down. I had survived the crisis, but my body had absorbed the cost. I was depleted, and healing did not require more insight; it required safety.

So I slowed down. I rested without apology. I moved with intention. Some days I placed my hand over my chest and said my own name out loud, reminding my body that it was safe now. Power did not leave me when I slowed down; it became inhabitable.

By the time I reached this point, one question kept returning: *Who was I before I made myself small?* The answer was both unsettling and freeing. I had always been capable; I had simply forgotten because capability had been safer than presence. I did not need to become someone new. I needed to stop disappearing inside what I could do.

Leaving The Commons was the moment I chose power that could live in my body without consuming it. The decision told my soul she mattered, and it told my future it was allowed to arrive. I walked away knowing that freedom was coming even though first there would be grief. But power, at last, no longer asked me to vanish in order to work.

That changed everything.

THE BOUNDARIES THAT SAVED ME

I had already been carrying more than any woman should have to hold when the bottom dropped out again. It was a Sunday night, and I received a call from a woman I barely knew. I had been out running errands when my phone rang. I had missed two calls from the same number the night before; I had assumed it was my former husband as the call came from a secondary number that I had seen before. So, when the phone rang this time, I answered.

But it was not him. It was a woman.

She said she was calling me woman to woman. Her voice was careful and measured. She told me her name, and then she told me something that dropped straight through my body and lodged in my chest.

She said my former husband had been sharing sexual videos of me that I had never consented to being shared outside of our marriage.

Her words did not land all at once. They moved slowly, heavily, as though my body needed time to register what my ears had heard. The woman did not offer proof, and she did not provide details. She only said enough to make one thing clear: a line had been crossed within me that could not be uncrossed.

I asked a few questions. She answered only what she was willing to answer. Then she ended the call.

By the time I pulled onto the freeway to drive home, my body had gone numb. Then the numbness turned into anger. This was not about a rumor or gossip—it was about his control reaching into a part of my life that should have been protected long after our marriage ended.

For years after our divorce was finalized, I had still tried to move with grace. I helped him when I could. I was thoughtful. I still showed up where it mattered for our children, I still handled things with care.

This was different.

Toward the end of our marriage, I had asked him to delete any sexual material he had of me on his phone. He dismissed my concern. At the time, I chose to let it go, even though I knew it could be used against me one day.

The call that night was the fulfillment of this very fear I had buried.

I felt exposed. I felt violated. I was furious that even years later, my sense of consent, privacy, and agency was still being managed and controlled by him.

This violation happened long after the relationship was over, and it showed me that separation does not automatically mean safety. In that moment I understood that if I did not stop it, it would never stop.

That was when the last thread of my silence snapped. Silence had been my most practiced skill—I had used it to keep peace, to preserve stability, and to protect what I believed was fragile. But now I understood that silence was not neutral. It was an agreement I was no longer willing to sign. I saw clearly that protecting my former husband—his image and what he represented—had been costing me my life. I had to choose: I could preserve the illusion of peace, or I could protect myself.

I trusted my discernment without asking anyone to confirm it. I chose myself.

I knew I could not prove what I had been told; I did not yet have evidence. Yet for the first time, I chose action over fear. I went to the police station and explained what had happened even though I couldn't press charges without proof.

No determination was made, and no formal action was taken, but that was not the point. What mattered was that I showed myself I was willing to speak, willing to stand up—willing to draw a line. When I came home from the police station, I did not react impulsively. I sat with my feelings.

Then I tried to follow up, but the woman who had called me disappeared from reach.

Eventually I had to address my former husband directly. I told him what I had been told and made it clear that it was unacceptable to me. He did not directly respond to what I shared; instead, he told me there were things we needed to talk about in person. It seemed to me that his response moved around the issue without resolving it.

In that moment I realized two things: clarity was not something I was going to receive, and I was no longer willing to stay in conversation without resolution. My boundary was no longer negotiable, and I did not need certainty to set that boundary. I needed safety.

I blocked him.

He no longer had access to me—to my energy, to my nervous system, or to my life. It was the first time in my adult life that his access to me ended completely.

This moment accelerated my reclamation. With that emotional cord finally severed, something in me came alive; I felt clarity where fear had lived. I had crossed a threshold I would never cross back over.

In the days that followed, I shifted gears. I was no longer waiting for the other shoe to drop, no longer managing someone else's volatility. There was a quiet I cannot fully explain, and there was power in my voice again. I learned that boundaries are not punishments; they are exits. And the boundary that saved my life did not stop at my phone. It moved inward—into my work, my money, my proximity, my identity, my attachments, and my obedience to systems that had trained me to shrink.

Leaving does not automatically teach you how to live freely. It only creates the space where that work can finally begin.

LEARNING TO LIVE FROM MY CENTER

I believed that once I told the truth and drew the line, my voice would know what to do. That clarity would continue to carry me forward, that the woman who survived rupture would instinctively know how to live from her center.

But a voice is not reclaimed only once. It is not a switch you flip; it must be practiced. The body must be retrained after years of bracing.

And so life offered me another lesson, not on a stage or in front of a camera, but in a quiet hotel room on the other side of the country. This was a moment where everything I thought I had reclaimed collided with the truth of what was still unhealed in me. Discovering yourself after divorce has plenty of highs and lows, but it can also be messy when it comes to love.

I am a lover at heart, intense and passionate. In the summer months a man messaged me. He seemed nice; he spoke to me, and I spoke back. I do not know what it is, but whenever I am out of town, I am much more friendly and inquisitive. I was traveling with my mom and sister, and this man and I were sending voice notes, kind of getting to know each other.

I learned he was about ten years younger than me, had several children, and had been married multiple times. I chat enough online to be able to sense whether or not I am interested, and I pay more attention to how something feels than to how it is being presented. Despite the conversation we were having, I did not feel settled. So, after about a weekend of back and forth, I sent him a message telling him I did not feel alignment for myself and wishing him well on his journey. I unfollowed him and continued with my life.

Toward the end of the year, however, he reached out again to share that he was hosting an event and to invite me to attend as a guest. I remember thinking, *I have not done an appearance in a while.* My travel, hotel, and meals would be covered. I would simply show up.

But I was living differently now. I was navigating the world as a single woman for the first time in decades, and that came with new considerations I was still learning how to name. Invitations felt different. Travel felt different. Being invited by a man required a level of discernment I had not needed before. I did not want to fly into town without really knowing what his expectations might be. I suggested we start talking again first, just to have more context. The last time we had spoken had been months earlier.

So, we talked, but the rhythm felt off. He would disappear for days, then respond briefly, then reappear again with questions. He spoke about wanting marriage, and he also shared that he was a pastor, which immediately complicated things for me given my history. The conversations felt awkward and disjointed, and I did not feel at ease.

By this point, though, I had agreed to attend. I chose to follow through, flying into town, where he had someone pick me up at the airport. Everything seemed fine. The driver took me by the venue where the event would be held, and I met a few staff members. Everything appeared to be in order, so I went back to the hotel.

My host suggested we grab dinner, which was fine with me. But then the timing kept shifting. Eight became nine, nine became ten while he said he was in the lobby helping other guests he had flown into town. Eventually he made his way up to my room. Since he had booked the room, I allowed him inside. After my divorce I had never had a man in my hotel room.

I remember pausing in that moment, acutely aware of the strangeness of it. *I am in a hotel room with a man.* The last time I had been in such close quarters with a man who was not my former husband, I was eighteen years old. I had been with the same person for decades, so this was unfamiliar territory for me. I sat there thinking, *What is life, that this man is in my room right now?*

We talked about life and everything else. I was sitting on the bed; across from me, he sat in a chair. And then, without warning, he asked, "What is your intention in being here? What do you want to happen tonight?"

I said, "I am here for the event. What should I want to happen tonight?"

He asked if I wanted to have sex with him.

My body went cold. Still. Shut down. I was not aroused or drawn toward him in any sexual way. I remember asking, "Is that how this works? You meet someone, they ask the question, and you are expected to say yes?"

He responded in the affirmative, as though it were normal.

I was suddenly aware that I was testing my own limits and boundaries in real time. I was not attracted to him, not moving in that direction. I was in my forties—and still, my body was unprepared to speak when something did not feel right.

Then he started telling me stories about different women and his experiences. I remember sitting there thinking, *Wow. This is really the way it is.* We kept talking. Then he said it was so late, that it would take him an hour to get back home, and that he had to be back in just a few hours—so he would stay the night.

Inside, I thought, *I do not want that.*

But I did not say anything.

He said he was going to grab some food. He left and came back with something to eat. We talked about random things until it was probably around two in the morning. While he had been gone getting food, I had jumped in the shower, then put my pajamas on. Long sleeves, long pants, my hair wrapped. I got into bed, fully covered, ready for sleep, even while he was eating and talking. Then he said it again, that it made more sense for him to stay because of the early morning and the drive.

My mind was racing. *How did I get myself into this situation?* I did not want to be with him. I did not want him in my room. *He should leave, now.*

But I did not say any of that out loud.

I froze.

He got up and went into the shower. When he came back, he did not have any clothes on.

He got into the bed with me. Naked.

I did not look at his body; I could not tell you today what it looked like. I was in shock considering what was transpiring in real time. Everything around me faded. I remember thinking, *I am not attracted to you. I do not want to be here. I want to leave my body. I want to get up and run. I want this to be over. I wish I had never come.*

I was terrified. It was too much emotion at once; I could see the path I wanted to take, and I could not move toward it. I wanted to tell him to get out of my room, but I couldn't.

He got closer and said, "Let's cuddle."

I said, "No. I do not want to cuddle you. You do not have any clothes on."

I drew an invisible line down the middle of the bed and told myself, *If I just lie here for a few hours, he will be gone and this will be over.* I tolerated the discomfort in my body because I did not speak up. I was trying to avoid conflict; I did not know him well, and I did not know how he would respond.

I lay there next to a naked man I was not attracted to in the middle of the night, feeling trapped. I was so still I could feel my heart pounding in my chest. I listened to the air conditioner hum. I felt sick to my stomach, deeply uncomfortable. The moment terribly violated my sense of safety— and at the same time, I turned the violation inward, blaming myself for not doing something to stop it.

This was the same freeze I had lived in during my marriage. *Do not blink. Just let it pass. Then you will be okay. Avoid conflict at all costs.*

It was the same silence I had learned as a little girl. *Do not provoke it. Do not make it worse. When you are hurt or disrespected, swallow it. Keep it inside.*

It was the same fear that someone would lash out, get angry, or that I would somehow be in trouble. Nothing was forced, but my consent was never freely given.

Morning came just a few hours later. He got dressed and left. The moment I heard the door close, I exhaled fully for the first time that night. I remember thinking, *Okay. I am safe.*

Then came the wave of emotion.

I felt embarrassed that I did not speak up. I felt shame. I felt violated. I felt like I had crossed a line with myself again, choosing peace over truth. To protect his comfort, I had waged a war inside my own body.

That night taught me that finding your voice is not a one-time event; it is a muscle that must be exercised. I could be powerful on a stage, I could be articulate in public, but alone with one person, I could not say, "I need you to leave. I am uncomfortable. I do not want you here."

After that night I changed my ticket to the earliest flight home. I promised myself I would never put myself in that position again. Defending myself mattered more than protecting someone else's feelings. At the time, I carried the weight of that night as if I had done something wrong. I replayed it in my mind, wondering why I had not spoken up more forcefully, why I had chosen silence over confrontation. But looking back now, I want to say something clearly for anyone reading this who has ever found themselves in a moment like that: what happened was not my fault. I did not invite it. I did not cause it. I did not deserve it. The responsibility for that night belongs entirely to the man who created it.

Later he messaged me. It became clear that whatever expectations he had were not aligned with what I had communicated or wanted. When I got home, I told him the situation had not been okay for me, that I was not comfortable with what had happened—that being in that bed, in that room, when I did not want to be there, was one of the most distressing nights of my life. I told him I wished he had left, and I also told him I wished I had spoken sooner.

It all made me realize how much of my voice still lived below my throat.

Around that same time, I hired a coach. I had been familiar with her online; she seemed confident, successful, and persuasive. One day she sent me a message and invited me to a small group session. I did not realize the session would include an invitation into a paid offer. I went in open, curious, hopeful. She spoke about strategy, alignment, legacy, and scale; she spoke in all the languages I was craving at that moment. Then she told me she offered private coaching for five thousand dollars. She said she would help me refine my vision, position my brand, and step into my next chapter. She even hinted that she was looking for someone to step into a future role with her.

I felt the familiar pull. The old reflex. The belief that I needed someone else to fully actualize what was inside me. I did hesitate—I told myself that if I gained nothing, I would be wasting my money. If she truly was who she presented herself to be, however, I had everything to gain. That is the logic I had used my entire life . . . yes, the same logic that had kept me in relationships where I carried more than my share.

I paid her, and we had a four-hour session. She listened to everything I dreamed of building, everything I wanted to reclaim, all that I felt stirring in me—and when the session ended, I walked away with barely two pages of notes.

Nothing that gave me a structure I could build from. Nothing that translated into a next step I could hold. I left feeling disappointed, a painfully familiar sensation.

Once again I had placed my becoming in the hands of someone who sounded powerful but was not equipped for what I needed. It was the same pattern I had lived in for years: I kept searching for someone who could be for me what I had always been to other people. I kept trying to recreate the dynamic where my worth was proven by how well I supported someone else or how well someone else could direct me. I still carried those codependent threads inside of me, those old beliefs that told me I was safer when someone else was in the lead.

What hurt the most was not the money I lost, it was the recognition of what I had done. I had allowed myself, again, to be positioned as the person believing instead of the architect. I could see other people clearly, but I struggled to see myself just as clearly, and in that gap I became vulnerable to the same dynamic in different forms: the promise of certainty, the pull of someone else's authority, and the temptation to hand my agency away in exchange for direction. I began to see how easy it is to confuse proximity to confidence with clarity.

How often we outsource our knowing when we are standing at the edge of our own becoming. How quickly authority replaces intuition when we are afraid to trust ourselves. Each of these encounters carried the same lesson for me: I did not need an external authority to become myself. Reclaiming myself meant breaking that belief in real time. It meant rising in my own agency, reminding myself that I had the power to build a life for myself, with myself, by myself. That had to become enough.

Maybe that is the deepest work of voice: not just speaking when you are ready, but speaking when you are afraid. Not just telling the truth when you are safe but learning to honor the truth while you are still in the room. Both of these encounters showed me the same truth from different angles: Voice is not performance. Voice is embodiment. Voice is the moment you stop waiting for permission and choose yourself first.

AWAY FROM EVERYTHING I KNEW

By the time this season arrived, I believed I had already done a great deal of healing. What I had not yet understood was that healing does not always announce itself through crisis. Sometimes it reveals itself quietly in what you stop chasing and what you finally allow to fall away.

After the divorce I did not date in the way I thought I would. I believed I was ready before I truly was; I was still tethered to the past in ways I could not yet see. My body carried memory—memory of what it meant to be chosen, memory of what it meant to belong, memory of love that felt intoxicating and love that felt dangerous, sometimes indistinguishable from each other.

Much of my deeper learning came through relationships with women. Old patterns surfaced there too, just without the intensity or illusion that had once kept me distracted. I knew, somewhere deep in my body, that I could not survive being broken by a man again. That kind of devastation might have taken something from me I was not sure I could recover.

Sometimes I would talk to someone on the phone for a week, maybe two, and then I would feel it clearly: *No. This does not feel warm. This does not feel right.* I would gently throw the fish back into the sea. I did not collect attention. When I went out with someone, I talked easily, I laughed, I was open, and still, something in me was searching, wanting to be completed. Wanting the electricity of those early moments to carry meaning.

No matter how healed I believed myself to be, however, my body kept responding to what was familiar. I attracted a type I no longer wanted: men who felt like I could complete their story. I knew, with growing clarity, that I did not want to be anyone's completion anymore. At some point I let that old dream die—the way I had believed love had to arrive, the story I thought it had to tell. The formula I had carried for years. I made peace with the idea that if it was just me and only me for the rest of my life, I would be okay. I had never said that honestly before.

People say the best time to meet someone is when you are no longer searching, and I was getting dangerously close to that place. I hadn't given up on love, but I had stopped waiting to be rescued. My birthday was coming up, and I asked myself a simple question: *What would you do if you were single?*

I would travel.

Turks and Caicos had lived on my list for years. I booked the flight and reserved the hotel. I did not make it a group trip, and I did not wait for company. I paid for the trip with savings I had quietly set aside, the kind you build when you have spent years holding everything together and learned how to survive uncertainty.

It was not an escape; it was a choice. For eighteen years I had celebrated my birthday with someone else. This time, I was celebrating myself.

When the day came to fly out, I felt giddy in a way I had not felt in years. There was no work involved, no children, no one to manage. Nothing to anticipate! It was just me and me. I filled every empty space with peace on purpose. I told myself, *I want to know you. I want to love you. I want to learn how to choose you without explanation.*

I arranged car service, and I booked an ocean view room. I scheduled massages without justification. I did not cut corners; I honored myself fully. On my birthday morning, I asked myself one simple question: *What do you want to do today?*

The answer came easily. *The spa. A long lunch. A beautiful dinner.*

When I arrived at the spa, the staff surprised me with a birthday cake made of towels, stacked carefully with a single candle on top. They gathered and sang. I stood there stunned, unexpectedly moved. I was being witnessed without effort, care offered to me without cost. After my massage I returned to my room and found *Happy Birthday* spelled in flowers across the bed. There were balloons and a bottle of champagne. I paused, wondering if someone had sent it, but no one had. The staff had done it on their own. There was even a small note: *Happy Birthday. We hope you have a special day.* I sat down and let myself receive it.

At lunch, after being seated by the water, I ordered without looking at the price. That night, under candlelight, there was another cake. I laughed softly at the excess of it all. The food was extraordinary, but the peace was deeper than pleasure. I realized I was not celebrating a day; I was celebrating my presence in my own life.

For so long joy had been paired with vigilance, and happiness had come with an expectation of loss. But here I was, waking up the next day, and everything was still good. No fires, no emergencies, no storm forming in the distance. The quiet gave me silence long enough to hear myself. Someone could have called my old life a success; it looked good on paper, but it slowly drained me. This life felt real. I was showing up as myself every day, and I liked her. I trusted her.

That night when I returned to my room, the housekeeping supervisor was placing another bottle of champagne. I laughed and told her I was not much of a drinker. She smiled and asked if she could make me hot tea instead. I said yes, and there she was, standing in my room, serving me tea on my birthday. I realized I had never experienced that level of care in my adult life. Everywhere I turned here, there was presence, there was attention, there was kindness without expectation. It felt like a quiet assurance: *You are held. And now, you know how to hold yourself.*

The next day I sat on the beach for hours. I listened to the waves; I let the wind move across my skin; I ate fruit slowly. I rocked in a chair by the shoreline, doing nothing, needing nothing. That was the lesson: attunement.

Turks and Caicos showed me that I did not need noise to feel alive, that joy did not require permission, and that choosing myself did not require collapse or explanation. I did not yet know how quickly that truth would be tested. I only knew that I had chosen myself without fear, and I carried that version of me back to the room the next morning, unaware that life was already reaching for my attention.

SHOW ME WHAT YOU HAVE LEARNED

I didn't know that the truest test of the life I was building would arrive without warning through a phone call that interrupted joy mid-breath—and asked me to stay present anyway.

It was the doctor's office. They told me they had received the results of my mammogram and needed me to come back for additional testing. They had noticed something abnormal.

It was only my second mammogram ever, and I remember thinking, *It is my birthday week! I am on a beach in Turks and Caicos. Why are you calling me like this?* But the woman on the phone explained calmly that I needed to schedule follow-up testing immediately.

I hung up and sat in silence. My old story tried to rise, saying there is always something bad that comes with the good—but I resisted it. I said out loud, "You were happy before that phone call. You get to choose if this moment steals your joy. You do have power over this feeling."

I stayed present, and I enjoyed the rest of the trip to the best of my ability. When I returned home, I understood something new: not only would I have to fight for myself, I would now have to comfort myself, walk with myself, and become my own anchor through whatever this next chapter held. I would be lying if I said I did not cry. Finding your voice and reclaiming your life is one kind of strength, but facing a possible cancer diagnosis alone is another kind entirely. As a former nurse, I knew what illness meant from the inside out. I thought, *Did all the stress finally catch up to me?*

I remembered my sister-in-law who died of brain cancer, and I remembered my stepmother-in-law who had breast cancer. I remembered the years in my marriage when I felt like my body was shutting down from sorrow. I had once believed I would die if I stayed—was this the bill coming due?

I left Turks and Caicos holding two opposing truths at once: I had just experienced the deepest pleasure of self-love I had ever known, and I was now walking toward one of the greatest uncertainties of my life. Turks and Caicos had shown me that I could celebrate myself and still be held even with fear in my body. This was the moment my feminine energy dropped from concept into embodiment. It was the softness after the storm, the pleasure after the pain. But life does not let you stay on the beach forever. Life called me back home with the mammogram results. That began the next layer of my becoming—the season where I had to learn how to mother myself, protect myself, and walk myself through uncertainty without abandoning who I had just become.

My follow-up doctor's appointment was scheduled for a week after I returned, and I was anxious. I also felt the ache of not having a partner to walk through this with me. I would have to face one of the most difficult health moments of my life alone. The only other times I had been hospitalized were for my two C-sections; I had always prioritized my health. Now I felt the absence of a spouse deeply because I wanted someone to come and be present with me.

I had a decision to make: sink into sadness over what I no longer have, or honor myself by becoming what I need? I did have family; I had my parents, my siblings, and my children, but I was used to an intimate partner. Now, instead, I had to be there for myself, speak life over myself. So I repeated to myself, over and over, *Myesha, you can do this. You can do hard things. You have suffered well. You know how to move through difficult seasons. And if this is part of your story, then so be it.* I became aware of how powerful our words are, and I began using that power to speak life over my body and my future.

There was no built-in community around me during this season of my life, so I learned to ask for what I needed. As the appointment approached, I went on Instagram and shared in my stories that I had received an abnormal mammogram result and needed further testing. I asked for prayer. The response overwhelmed me. I cried. The kindness my followers expressed to me meant that my life mattered, my work mattered. I could still be held by my digital community even in vulnerability. Women reached out to me, sending me their stories, prayer messages, and encouragement. I realized that embodied healing means allowing yourself to be seen in your need, not just in your strength. Being my own person meant being responsible for my own care *and* letting people support me.

My journey was not linear; there were peaks and sudden detours, and this was a detour I never saw coming. One of my deeper fears surfaced—cancer—but instead of collapsing under it, I became my own protector, my own covering, my own advocate. I learned how to rescue myself and then how to allow others to stand with me. I taught others how to care for me by modeling it first: I began waking earlier, taking longer baths, going to Pilates, and eating with more intention. I placed myself back at the center of my own life. My health mattered, my sleep mattered, and my thought life mattered. I became more intentional with both my mornings and my nights, with my grooming, my home, my room, and my rest. I stopped waiting for someone else to tend to me and began tending to myself, and I noticed something powerful: as I met my own needs, I stopped feeling ashamed of having them.

For most of my life, I had met my own needs out of a need to survive, because no one else would. Now, when the day finally came to walk back into that doctor's office, I did not enter as a wife, a caregiver, or a shadow of who I had once been. I walked in as a woman holding herself, protecting herself, and speaking life over her own body.

Even with all the self-mothering, all the prayers, all the baths, and all the rewiring, the morning of the appointment still arrived like a storm. I felt the familiar urge to reach for someone else's covering, to ask for prayer, to be held in a way I no longer was. My body still remembered what it meant to be led through moments like this. But I let the impulse pass. I gathered myself instead.

I parked the car. I let the kids know. *Pray for me. Think of me.*

And then I went in alone.

The waiting room was cold and moderately crowded as I filled out the paperwork. Every kind of emotion lived in that room. This was not a happy place. I was led to a private changing room and given instructions to take off my shirt and put the cape on. Open in the front, just like last time.

The technician said we would do the mammogram first. If they did not see anything, I would be free to go home. If they did see something, they would do additional testing. Then the machine pressed and squeezed and compressed until it felt unbearable. Afterward, the attendant told me to wait in the hallway about ten minutes while she showed the doctor the images. They would see where we went from there.

I went and sat down.

Worship music was playing. I started fighting back tears when I heard it; I could feel God with me. I had this quiet knowing that everything was going to be okay, and at the same time, I was terrified.

I used to work on the cancer ward as a nurse tech and as a nursing student. It broke my heart; being with people at the end of their lives was one of the saddest experiences I had ever known as a deeply empathetic person. All of it came rushing back while I sat there waiting for results. Those ten minutes felt like an hour. I trambled, thinking about life, thinking about every person in that room. It hit me that everyone there was waiting for the next chapter of their life to be decided as well.

The silence was heavy. No one was talking. There was no chitchatting. Just waiting.

Then the technician came back. She told me they saw something on my left breast, so they needed to do more tests.

I stood in that hallway alone and thought, *I am just a kid. I don't know how to do this.* And the truth was, I didn't. Not as this version of me, not without the familiar scaffolding I had leaned on for years.

That's when I realized the woman I had become was here, but the little girl inside me was here too. Both of us had walked into that room. Both of us were scared. Both of us were praying the other could be strong enough. I became childlike instantly when the nurse spoke to me; I wanted to disappear. I thought, *This is too hard. I need someone to be strong for me.*

But I told her okay, and—fighting back tears, looking up at the ceiling—I went in for the ultrasound.

They scanned every angle. Every quadrant. I asked so many questions. The nurse in me rose up—*Are you sure? How many people review this? What are you looking for? Where are you looking? How can this be?*

After what felt like forever, the doctor came in and said my ultrasound technician was one of the best, that the women's center where I'd done the testing used some of the best technology in the area, and that I should be confident in what they were telling me. Then she said that while they had seen something on the mammogram, they did not see it on the ultrasound. They wanted me to go home and live my life and come back in six months.

The relief hit me like a wave—overwhelming. I was still questioning; fear always wants to be fed. But I chose not to feed it. I told myself, *In this present moment, there is nothing to be afraid of.* I let everyone know that for now, everything was okay, and I would return in six months for follow-up. Even then, I tried to hold gratitude gently, knowing that someone else in that same waiting room did not receive relief. I felt the heaviness lift from my body as I walked out because I could still feel the heaviness that remained on everyone else.

I went into that office one woman, and I walked out another.

That's the thing about a health scare: the appointment ends, but the echo of it doesn't. You walk out relieved, grateful, alive, and yet marked. Something inside you rearranges itself. Something inside you decides, *I'm not wasting another minute of this life.* That six-month wait became its own teacher, its own mirror. It asked me who I wanted to be with the time I had left, however long that was.

That became the beginning of a new chapter. Choosing myself was no longer a philosophy. It was a practice, one I would return to again and again.

WHEN I LET MYSELF WANT

After the initial fear passed, what remained was a question. It felt like do-or-die—I wasn't in danger, but I could feel my life closing in on itself. There were no more threats around me; I had set the boundaries I needed to set, and my life was quiet and peaceful. Then, right on cue, panic rushed in and said, *You need to hurry. You need to do something. Nobody is going to take care of you. What are you going to do?*

I recognized that voice. It had kept me alive for a long time.

I had watched my parents and grandparents work their entire lives, retire, and call that safety. I knew that path; I knew the outcome. I had already invested twenty years of my life into something that would no longer serve my future, but I still had time to choose differently, and I desired to create a life that I wanted to live from the inside out. After all, there was no one left to blame. My marriage was over, and the church was behind me. The excuses to continue to put it off were gone. There were dreams and visions I had carried since I was a child, and I reached a moment that said this clearly: Either you step forward and build the life you want, or you choose what is safe and predictable and accept the outcome that path always gives.

I was in my early forties, however, and I remember thinking, *You could put in another twenty-five years. You could get a pension, you could pay your rent, and you could survive respectably.* But in my body a different question kept echoing: *What was all of that for? What did I go through all of this for if I am just going to end up right back where I started?*

I said, *No. I need time and space to create the life I want to live. I am not letting fear set the terms anymore.* I was by myself, walking my tenth lap around the park, when I said it out loud: "I am betting it all on me."

If I have learned anything in this life, it is that my days must reflect what I value. I was done with what impresses others or looks responsible on paper. I only wanted what sustained me. Fear kept saying, *You need stability. You need to know what you are going to have.* But something steadier answered back: *I am tired of breadcrumbs. I am tired of just enough. I am tired of settling for consistency when only I am the consistent one. I am not going to abandon myself. I make good choices, and I can trust myself.* The scariest question was not, "What if it does not work?" It was, "What if it works better than I ever imagined? What if everything I have lived through was preparation for this?"

All said and done, I bought my freedom and took a gap year.

It was about sovereignty—living with less certainty than I had ever known and more alignment than I ever had. I wasn't chasing optics or approval; I did not need anyone to look at my life and decide I was doing okay. Instead, I asked different questions: What does it actually take for me to live? What is the bare minimum I need so that the rest of my life can be mine?

Once I asked that honestly, the answers came quickly. I realized I could not keep carrying the symbols of a life I had outgrown. I was surrounded by things that once spoke for me—objects that had once told the world I was safe, successful, chosen, enough—and they were suddenly quiet. I had learned how to assemble worth, how to curate it, how to wear it: bags, jewelry, cars. The shorthand that speaks before you do. Those things had served me once. I do not shame that woman; she was surviving. But survival was no longer the assignment.

I remember the day I decided. Standing in my house, I said it out loud. "No more." I had a new identity, and this version of me no longer required external validation.

I gathered the jewelry: The Cartier bracelet. The Van Cleef bracelet I'd received for Mother's Day. The diamonds. The watches. I carried them all to the jeweler myself, and I placed each piece on the counter. I signed the paperwork, and they handed me a check.

And I felt exhilarated.

I had finally let go of luxury, releasing a version of worth I no longer needed. I took that check to the bank and knew I was funding my future with alignment, not performance.

Around the same time, I sold my car. After my divorce, buying that Mercedes Coupe had felt like reclamation. It told the world I was still whole, still powerful, still living well. For a while I needed that—until I didn't.

I sold it and bought a Toyota Prius. For the first time in my adult life, I had no car payment—no pressure, and no image to maintain. I wanted financial space, and space meant things working for me, not me working for things.

I also downsized my home. My family had been used to everyone having their own room, their own bathroom, their own complete privacy. Extra living space had become normal, and comfort had become standard. I had been proud of that house; it was a visible symbol of what I believed I had built, a multi-million-dollar home in a sprawling gated community. I did it by myself. *I* did that. That house felt like proof that although I was a single mother, I was capable. Proof that I could create security, that I could sustain a life that looked successful from the outside.

But it was built for a version of me that no longer existed.

Choosing to leave it was not a financial decision alone. It was also an identity decision. I moved somewhere less expensive and more aligned with the season I was actually in. The new house did not impress; it did not stretch to fill expectations. It fit. I was rebuilding, and rebuilding requires honesty about where you are, not attachment to where you once stood. Everything I let go of became seed money for my freedom. I never repurchased those things, though it wasn't because I couldn't; I did not need to. What I needed most was more emotional space. Space to write, space to create, space to build in my own rhythm. I wanted the ease of lowered expectations and true peace.

My days became quieter. I woke up early while the air was still cool. I walked, I created, and I made sure my daughter got to school. I checked on my son. I worked with my clients. Some days I did nothing at all. Sometimes I traveled.

At first, the stillness felt unfamiliar. Then I realized it was peace. I remember driving to the car wash one morning: windows down, music playing, mountains in front of me. Tears welled up in my eyes. I hadn't arrived somewhere impressive; I had finally arrived inside myself. For the first time my life felt authored instead of inherited.

Looking out over the mountains, I whispered to myself, *You did it.*

You made it.

INTEGRATION

UNTETHERED

Freedom often scares us before it steadies us. When I stopped needing approval, the scaffolding of my life disappeared. So many of my adult relationships had been built on being needed, on being reliable, on being the one who answered first, carried the most, and absorbed the weight so others did not have to. That was what I had been affirmed for in my marriage. That was what I had been praised for in church. For a long time, that was where my worth lived.

When that approval was no longer required, the structure that had organized my life collapsed. It did not shatter in one dramatic moment; it unraveled in silence. Without the roles that once defined me, I was left face-to-face with a question I had never had to ask before: Could I continue to spend the rest of my life alone and be okay?

That question arrived as an opening.

Sometimes starting over is not brave. It is humiliating. No one prepares you to rebuild a life you believed was already built. To me it felt like standing under bright lights while someone read my history back to me, a public audit of every decision that led here: the marriage, the moves, the ministry, the investments, the image, and the house. It made me realize that "someday plans" don't transfer.

"One day we will buy that house.

"One day we will retire."

"One day we will travel the world together."

I had been speaking in future tense for years without realizing how dependent I was on it. Those plans had shape. They had furniture; they had color palettes and savings accounts and calendars attached to them, but they belonged to a version of my life that no longer existed. I did not just lose a marriage or a career or a church; I lost the ecosystem that made my life make sense. The rhythms of shared routines, the shorthand language—even the way decisions were once made with a "we" instead of an "I." Overnight everything had shifted at once: a new home, a new faith, different friends, different work, a new body, a different self. People call that reinvention, but it felt more like disorientation, like stepping onto land that looks solid but moves beneath you, like learning to walk again in shoes that do not yet feel like yours.

There were days it felt like proof of failure, like evidence of years I wished I could rewrite. I would look at the life I had built and feel the ache of having to leave it. I was proud of that life; I had fought for it, paid for it, maintained it, and protected it. And now I was in a new life. The humiliation is not loud; it is quiet. It is explaining your new address, it is answering questions without actually answering them, and it is watching people recalculate who you are in real time.

And still. Staying would have cost me my soul. That became undeniable.

Starting over was not a performance of strength; it was an act of preservation. It was the only way to keep something intact inside of me that was more important than reputation, comfort, or continuity. Freedom is expensive. I paid for it with certainty, with comfort, and with the story I thought I was living. I paid with the image that once protected me. I paid with the illusion that if I just endured long enough, everything would make sense again.

Some days it felt like loss. Some days it felt like peace. Most days it was both at the exact same time. This is what untethering actually feels like: it feels like standing in the middle of what used to be solid and realizing you are still standing anyway.

During that season I began a quiet practice. I imagined myself near the end of my life, looking back at this moment, and asked one question: *What decision will I be most proud of having made?* The answer was never the safe one. It would have been easy to choose comfort, to get a job that paid the bills, to make life predictable again. There is nothing wrong with stability, but I knew that if I reached the end of my life and all I could say was that I had kept everything intact—that I had avoided disruption, that I had protected appearances—it would not be enough for me. I wanted my future self to know that I had trusted myself when there was no blueprint, that I had listened when something inside me refused to be negotiated away, and that I had chosen alignment over applause.

Freedom, I learned, is not philosophical. Eventually, it asks for proof, and that proof arrived when I was offered work that made perfect sense on paper. I had the credentials, the experience, and the capacity, but it was the kind of work that would have rewarded the version of me who disappears inside duty. I knew exactly how to step in, how to stabilize the system, how to hold everything together quietly, and I could feel the old reflex rising in me, ready to perform competence, ready to rescue, ready to anchor something that was not mine to carry. Saying yes would have solved immediate problems, but saying no meant trusting a future I could not yet see.

I said no. And when I put the phone down, I felt relief. The kind that settled in my chest and told me that I did not betray myself this time.

Agency, I learned, is sure of itself. It is the decision you make when no one is watching and the refusal to rebuild your life around the same patterns that once required your disappearance. Untethered, for me, did not mean ungrounded. It meant I got to choose my anchors. I was no longer living inside systems that told me who I was; I was authoring my life in real time. I did not have everything I once believed I needed, but for the first time, I had something I had never fully possessed before: a life that was actually mine.

Starting over is not glamorous. It is grief and liberation sharing the same body; it is shaking and steady at once. It is fear and clarity holding hands and choosing yourself anyway.

If you are rebuilding in midlife, you did not miss your life.

You refused to keep living the wrong one.

STAY

For decades Easter Sunday had been one of the most demanding days of the year for me. The buildup alone was exhausting: outfits chosen in advance, services multiplied, venues rented, and rooms expanded to make space for more people, more expectation, more performance. Our family arrived early and stayed late, and by the time the day had ended, I was always empty in a way I did not know how to name.

A few years after leaving that life, Easter came once again, and I realized I had not been inside a church on Easter in a long time. Almost immediately after this thought, the old reflex surfaced: *It is Easter. You should go to church.*

I thought about what I would wear and which church I would even attend. Where would I sit? That familiar, unspoken question rose again, one I had lived with for years as a pastor's wife: *Where do I belong now?*

Then, quietly, I chose something else. That morning I stayed home. I slept in, and I ordered French toast and had it delivered. I sat in my bed and ate slowly, without rushing, preparing, or being needed.

There was no music swelling. No stage. No agenda.

Just me.

I took time to reflect on my relationship with God as it had actually been lived: the one that carried me through grief, silence, and unlearning rather than imposing obligation or visibility. I noticed how different it felt to be grateful without performing, to be present without producing anything in return.

Later that afternoon, I went for a long walk. The air was soft, the sky was open, and the sun lowered itself toward the horizon without asking anything of me. I thought about what Easter represents. It is not spectacle, but resurrection. Resurrection does not require a building. It requires presence.

That day mattered because I had done the honest thing. I was not hiding from God. I was choosing alignment and honoring the season I was in instead of forcing myself into one I had outgrown. That Easter taught me something I had not known how to trust before: that reverence can be quiet, that devotion can look like rest, and that presence can be enough.

This is what it meant to be untethered. Instead of rushing to attach myself to something familiar, I stayed in the in-between space. It was not a place of emptiness, but one of integration. It is where old identities fall silent and something truer has room to emerge.

This was not the end of my becoming; it was the ground beneath it. For a long time healing had been my lifeline. It gave me shape when my life lost form. Now another gentle question emerged: *If I was no longer broken, who was I becoming?*

BECOMING SOMEONE I'VE NEVER MET BEFORE

Healing gave me language when my community disappeared. It gave me connection when everything else went quiet, and it gave me belonging when I had lost everything else. I've always had a growth mindset; I loved the books, the practices, the questions. Eventually, however, I noticed something subtle and important: I was always reaching outward. Fixing, repairing, searching. I had to accept the truth I had been avoiding: everything I needed was already within me. There was nothing left to fix. There was no woman who was devastated, bankrupt, or incomplete. She was whole and she was standing, right here.

I had to release the identity of being the woman who was healing.

Once, after I said out loud that I had healed, someone corrected me. "You're never quite healed," they said. But I knew what I meant. I wasn't claiming perfection; I was naming completion. I had put the pieces where they belonged for now. I was no longer living in a perpetual state of repair.

This was harder than I expected because I had built community around healing. It was how I connected with other women. Everywhere I went, someone would whisper, *I'm going through a divorce,* and suddenly we were bonded in a corner, sharing our stories. Letting go of that identity meant I wasn't open to those conversations in the same way anymore. I had moved into a different phase of my life. I had already left the role of pastor's wife—marriage, church, and everything that defined me before—

and without realizing it, I had gone on to pick up a new role: the healing woman. The woman doing the work. Now I had to let go of that too.

Yet, when I stopped fixing myself, a deep peace settled in. I wasn't a project; I was a person. People relate differently to a person than they do to a project. Messages came that I didn't answer right away, invitations to things I turned down and didn't rush to explain. I let silence hold what urgency used to carry. At the same time, healing had focused my attention, given me purpose when my sense of meaning had collapsed. I told myself maybe this was why I had gone through it all—to help others, to tell my story, to keep sharing. And then one day, I ran out of things to say.

That silence scared me more than the pain ever had. I had done what I needed to do. What now?

What I feared most was becoming irrelevant again. If I wasn't clinging to this identity, who would I be? How would I be of service? So I turned inward and began asking a different question: instead of wondering, *How can this help others?* I thought, *How can I live well with what I've been given?*

For the first time in my life, it didn't matter who saw me. It didn't matter how visible I was. All that mattered was that I was proud of the woman I was becoming. I started living by a simple rule: if I couldn't see myself doing something five years from now, I wouldn't do it today. It wasn't discipline, it was discernment.

Another realization followed. For as long as I could remember, I had felt responsible for being "the one"—the star, the person who made it. I had been searching for significance, visibility, importance, and power my entire life. I didn't want a quiet life; I wanted to be seen. Then something shifted. One evening, walking through the park as the sun was setting, I finally felt the truth: if no one ever knows me, if no one validates my work or sees what I've built, I am okay. And this time, I meant it.

A tear welled up because that desire had once defined me. Now, suddenly it was gone. I had a life I loved; I owned my days and my body. I had agency, direction, and clarity. I had paid a price for this life, and I didn't need anyone outside of me to tell me I was worthy.

I stopped generating meaning through performance and started generating it from within. My sleep deepened, and my creativity came back. Joy followed. I realized how much of my life had been a trauma response, a constant reaching for what I didn't receive early on. I became someone I had never met before: someone integrated.

I noticed it in my decisions when I moved with clarity. I stopped overthinking; I trusted my own wisdom. I waited when I needed to, and I acted when it was time. I stopped performing for my family. I stopped saving and compensating and explaining.

I also stopped talking about what happened. Being a divorced woman had become part of my identity, and it was tethering me to the past. Now I had crossed a threshold. I didn't want to live there anymore.

I deleted the dating apps. My urgency to be seen faded. My motivation to post online quieted. I came home to myself, and in that stillness, something unexpected happened: I didn't need to be famous anymore. I didn't need to be important.

I became devoted to living inside my own life, walking in real shoes, and making ordinary days meaningful. Dreaming dreams that stretched beyond what I had once imagined. I wasn't fixing anymore. I wasn't preparing for a future version of myself.

I was here.

THE COLLEGE DROP-OFF

It was the summer, and my eldest daughter had decided in July that she wanted to go to college in the fall. She had originally planned to go to community college, but now she was changing her mind and wanted to attend a university out of state. She applied and was accepted to four out of five four-year institutions.

Everything moved fast after that. We had about four weeks before school started to complete everything. She had to pick the school, and we had to finalize finances, set her class schedule, choose her dorm, and get everything set up. It was a blur of online portals and emails and deadlines. Boxes began to pile up, lists were written and rewritten. Her room started to empty out slowly without me quite realizing it. There is something disorienting about watching your child move toward their life while you are still standing in yours.

At some point in the middle of all of it, she mentioned that she wanted her dad to come with us to drop her off. I gave her the flight itinerary that I had already booked for her, myself, and my youngest daughter so she could pass it along to him, and I remember thinking, *I am going to spend four days near somebody that I have not been around in years, and we are going to have to be in close company.*

Originally I felt okay about it. I had done my work, and there was not one part of me that was looking for anything. I genuinely thought, *This is the best thing for her, so it will be fine.*

It was fine, but it was not effortless.

There were moments during the trip when my body responded before my thoughts did. I found myself reaching for chocolate late at night and sugar during the day: small comforts. I was subconsciously doing more to regulate myself. It was strange to realize that my mind no longer led these moments; my body did. Quietly, subtly, without asking permission. I did not judge it. I did not correct it. I paid attention.

Discomfort does not always announce itself; sometimes it shows up in appetite, in restlessness, or in the need for something sweet to take the edge off a memory you are no longer living inside. That week taught me that healing does not erase response, but it does change how we meet it. What I was noticing, without needing to name it yet, was my capacity. I could be in proximity to my former spouse without being destabilized, and I could feel discomfort without collapsing or reaching for old strategies to manage it. I did not need to perform calm or convince myself I was okay. I simply was.

My interactions with him that week showed me a lot about the woman I had become. The old me would have planned all the flights and made sure he booked his hotel. The old me would have handled everything subtly and carried the weight without asking anyone else to participate fully, but the new me gave the information to my daughter and made sure she communicated directly with her dad about what needed to happen.

I still took a leadership role like I always do; I still made sure my children and I got to where we needed to go, and I educated myself on what would happen there. But I noticed something important: the woman I had become was not a pushover. She was intentional and passionate, but she had boundaries.

Yet my body remembered what it had been like to be around him before my mind had time to assess—the kind of memory that lives below language. I noticed it in small ways. My shoulders stayed slightly lifted. My jaw held tension longer than usual. I felt alert in a way I had not felt in years. But I registered it quietly. I did not make extra meaning out of it; I simply noticed that my body was still learning how to stand in proximity to something it once had to manage.

That awareness alone told me how far I had come. That week showed me that I had really done the work.

I used to feel like I was walking around on eggshells; there was a constant anticipation of disruption. I moved carefully so I would not contribute to anything exploding in my life. On the outside, I appeared calm, but on the inside, I often felt like a volcano waiting to erupt. In this season, however, I no longer waited for the other shoe to drop. The peace I went to sleep in was the peace I woke up in. I had stabilized my nervous system enough to experience calm most of the time, and even when something disruptive did happen, I had prepared myself so well that it did not knock me out of alignment.

Before, discomfort had always meant action: fix it, smooth it, anticipate it. This time discomfort asked nothing of me. I could let it exist without it controlling me. My body already knew how to process and diffuse it.

I slept deeply, enjoying meaningful rest. I used to hold so much stress in my neck, and my jaw was always tight, my body always braced. Now I felt relaxed, as though I had lost ten years of weight. I had stopped needing to change who I was. I no longer needed to be small. I stopped adjusting my conversation, and I stopped making other people seem bigger so I could stay smaller.

I began to notice things I had overlooked for twenty years: I would see the sun shining, feel the breeze, and would pause and sit at the park just to hear the kids play—to listen to their laughter, to the swing moving back and forth, and to families talking while they grilled food and shared a meal together. I was fully present in my life.

There was grief in the transition, even as everything felt right. I quietly grieved being needed as the one who held everything together. I grieved the identity that told me my value came from making life easier for someone else. That story had lived in me for a long time; to be needed had meant I mattered, and letting go of that identity meant stepping out of a role I had rehearsed my entire life.

But I was sturdy now, and there was no negotiating. If you could not meet me where I was, you no longer had access to me.

That clarity carried its own loneliness. After everything was done with the move—after the boxes were unpacked and the bed was made and the room began to look like hers instead of temporary living quarters, my daughter stood there and looked at me. She said, "Thank you, Mom. I know how to organize and make things happen because of you."

I smiled and hugged her, but later, when I was alone, it settled in: her beginning meant releasing the version of myself who had been needed to do it all for her—the mother who tracked every detail, who anticipated everything before it was asked, and whose care lived in constant readiness. Instead, I could let her step forward without orchestrating the transition. I could trust what I had already given her.

That night, when it was time to leave, she walked us down to the parking lot. The air was cooler than it had been earlier, the campus quieter. We stood beside the car, none of us rushing the moment, all of us aware that this was the end of what we had known.

She hugged her sister. She hugged her dad. I stood still and watched, giving her the space to say her goodbyes in her own way. I remember taking a slow, deliberate breath, steadying myself in it. I had done this before. I had let go before.

But this felt different. This was not loss. This was expansion.

When she turned to me, I held her a little longer. I said, "I am so proud of you," and I meant it. I was so proud of the resilience she had built, proud of the healing she had fought for, and proud of the way she had stayed soft after everything she had endured.

I was not losing my daughter. I was watching her step fully into her own life—and in doing so, I felt myself stepping more fully into mine.

Life was changing shape again. This time, I did not resist it. I let the moment be exactly what it was.

FINALLY FREE

I woke up craving an oat milk latte and drove to one of my favorite places overlooking the ocean. The morning was bright and crisp with the kind of light that makes everything feel newly washed. I sat near the rail with the waves breaking below me, the sun warming my skin, the cup warm in my hands. I took a sip and smiled. This was the sweetness of life.

I looked out over the water and let my mind wander back over the years that had brought me here. If my eighteen-year-old self could see this life, I don't know that she would recognize it as the one she imagined. And yet, sitting there, something in me knew it had been purposeful.

There was a great deal that had to be shed along the way: the identities I once depended on to survive, being needed, being chosen, and being admired. None of those desires were wrong; they were rooted in something sincere and human. They simply carried more weight than they were meant to bear.

I thought about my life as it was now, what it felt like to live inside my own skin at last. How my body moved through the world, and how decisions came more clearly. How I could sense when something aligned and when it did not. A small smile appeared without effort.

It had all been worth it. Every single part of it.

I had built a beautiful life once—everything I thought I wanted, until it began to cost me myself. Losing it felt devastating at the time, but now I could see that what emerged in its place was truer than anything I had known before.

My chest felt soft. My breath moved easily. My eyes felt open and bright. My life was far from perfect, but it was mine. I knew who I was. I trusted myself. I could prioritize what mattered and release what did not. I could say no without guilt. I could walk away without explaining. I could choose the path that honored my nervous system, my values, my children, and my future. I had agency. I had individuality. I had choice. I could speak honestly. I could create without fear. I could love deeply without disappearing. I could be passionate, sensitive, hopeful, and grounded. I could be myself without bracing for consequence.

I was a free woman.

Freedom did not arrive as fireworks or applause. It arrived as steadiness, as coherence—as the quiet confidence of knowing that nothing essential could be taken from me again. There were moments now when I wanted to run and dance and shout; I felt liberated from the inside out. It was as if everything else had burned down to rubble—the structures, the assumptions, the identities I had clung to—and instead of trying to salvage what was broken, I had decided to rebuild. Brick by brick. Intentionally. I took pieces of myself and placed them back where they belonged. I reconsidered what mattered most, and I released what never really did. The inside of my body felt calibrated again. My thoughts, my emotions, and my instincts were no longer at war with each other.

I did not do this reinvention perfectly, and I did not rebuild flawlessly. I did it authentically. In this season of my life I learned that it is possible to enjoy the skin you are in, that I did not have to live in fear. The sun could shine brightly without my waiting for something to go wrong.

Some days I still find myself unexpectedly emotional, and tears come without warning. Nothing is collapsing, nothing is broken; it is simply a human response. It is grief moving through a body that has survived, joy arriving without armor.

For a long time, I thought I should wait to write this book. I imagined finishing it when I had the perfect house, or when I was married again, or merely when I was in love. I wanted my story to end in a way that felt cinematic.

But as I sat with that desire, I realized something: this may not be the ending I once imagined, but it is the truest one. I am still in-process. Still becoming. Sometimes I am still surprised by the version of myself that is emerging. I realized I did not need to wait until everything looked complete; I needed to exist honestly in the middle of it.

The fact that my heart is beating and I am alive is proof enough that rebuilding is possible. I did not check the boxes handed to me when I did so; I did not consult popular culture for its definition of success, and I did not measure my life against someone else's timeline. I trusted myself. I defined my own values for a life well-lived. And I am at peace.

Before I knew it, it was Christmas Eve.

My eldest daughter was home from her first semester of college, rejoining my son and youngest daughter, and the house felt full again. Vanilla-scented candles burned, the oven preheated, and Christmas music played through the speakers.

I cooked slowly that day—gumbo, the kind of meal that asks you to stay with it. I chose the crab carefully, standing at the stove, patient with the roux, chopping vegetables by hand, letting the house fill with warmth and familiar scent. I placed some wrapped gifts beneath the tree one by one as an act of care rather than effort.

At some point the music grew louder, and I started dancing and singing without thinking about it. The moment was perfect. My body felt light. The kids gathered around the island, and we danced. We laughed—the type of laughter that only comes when no one is bracing. And we sang.

We moved about in rhythm and harmony, and a memory surfaced: a picture from years earlier, during my plant medicine journey. I had been in a kitchen filled with movement and music, witnessing a life that felt whole and alive. I had once seen it only in flashes, in longing, but that night, I realized I was standing inside it.

It was real.

It rained all day—the first rain in a long while—but nothing touched the warmth in that room. My parents came over, and my sisters, my brothers, and my nieces. Family friends endured the weather to celebrate with us. Conversation moved easily; the laughter in the room rose and fell without effort. Bowls filled with gumbo were passed around the table with fresh garlic bread right out of the oven. Spoons clinked softly against ceramic, and someone commented on how good it was. A Christmas movie played in the background, half-watched, familiar, comforting. The house sounded alive. The afternoon couldn't have been more memorable.

Then the doorbell rang. It was my former husband.

We opened the door and welcomed him in. In that moment, past and present occupied the same room with ease, sharing warmth, conversation, and the ordinary rhythm of breath.

I stood in my kitchen serving: Steady. Present. At ease in my own skin. This was my life, and it did not require explanation. Nothing had to return to what it had been for it to feel complete.

That night, surrounded by my children, my family, and my history and my future sharing space, I understood something without needing to name it: I was fully alive.

This is not the life I had imagined while surviving. It is the life I built by choosing myself.

And it is honest.

ACKNOWLEDGMENTS

This book exists because of many hands, many moments, and many unseen forms of support.

To my children, thank you for your patience, your laughter, and the ways you held me steady when I was still learning how to stand. You are the reason I chose honesty over ease.

To my family, thank you for riding with me, and for giving me the freedom to become.

To the women who trusted me with their stories along the way, thank you for reminding me that healing is never solitary.

To the editors, collaborators, and creative partners who helped shape this work, thank you for your care, your discernment, and your respect for the integrity of the story.

To God, who remained when so much else fell away, thank you for holding me steady.

And finally, to the woman I was when this journey began: thank you for surviving long enough to become someone new.

ABOUT THE AUTHOR

Myesha Chaney is a writer, speaker, and coach whose work centers on honesty, reinvention, and the courage it takes to rebuild a life after it has come undone. Through her writing and speaking, she gives language to experiences many people carry quietly, including loss, identity shifts, spiritual disillusionment, divorce, and the long road back to oneself.

Over the course of her career, Myesha has led organizations and built businesses while helping others navigate seasons of growth and transformation. After years spent building a life that looked whole from the outside, she found herself navigating profound personal change that required her to dismantle old identities and rebuild from the ground up.

Her work now explores what it means to tell the truth about our lives, reclaim our voice, and begin again with clarity and self-trust.

Myesha is the author of *Honest: A Memoir of What I Built, What I Lost, and Who I Became* and *Hiding Behind the Lipstick.* As a coach, she works with individuals navigating major life transitions. A through line in all her work is helping people move beyond performance and step into a more honest and integrated life.

Myesha lives in California with her family.

To learn more about her work, visit
myeshachaney.com